WATER MIRROR REFLECTING HEAVEN

collected writings of

Tripitaka Master Hsuan Hua

Translated into English by
Dharma Realm Buddhist University
Buddhist Text Translation Society
Talmage, California ❀ 1982

WATER MIRROR REFLECTING HEAVEN

Written by Venerable Tripitaka Master Hsüan Hua
Translated by Bhikshuni Heng Tao
Reviewed by Bhikshuni Heng Ch'ih
Edited by Upasika Kuo Tsai (Susan) Rounds
Certified by Master Hua Bhikshuni Heng Wen

COPYRIGHT c 1982 BY THE SINO-AMERICAN BUDDHIST
    DHARMA REALM BUDDHIST UNIVERSITY

PRINTED IN THE UNITED STATES OF AMERICA
First printing: November 4, 1982, Anniversary of
Kuan Yin Bodhisattva's Leaving the Home-Life

ACKNOWLEDGEMENTS:

cover design & calligraphy, typing and layout by
    Shramanerika Heng Liang
proofing by Bhikshunis Heng Chü, Heng Cheng, Heng
Bin, Upasikas Kuo Lü Cole, Kuo Tsai Rounds, Kuo
Ts'an Nicholson
                    *****
FOR INFORMATION AND BOOKSALES CONTACT:

GOLD MOUNTAIN MONASTERY , 1731 -15th Street,
    San Francisco, Ca. 94103   (415) 861-9672
                              (415) 626-4204
GOLD WHEEL TEMPLE, 1728 West 6th Street, Los
    Angeles, Ca. 90017   (213) 483-7497
                        (213) 258-6177
CITY OF TEN THOUSAND BUDDHAS, Box 217, Talmage,
    California, 95481   (707) 462-0939
                       (707) 462-9945

ISBN   0-88139-501-3

南無本師釋迦牟尼佛

Namo Shakyamuni Buddha

TABLE OF CONTENTS

WATER MIRROR REFLECTING HEAVEN

宣公上人德相

慈悲普度信者得救成正覺

過化存神禮之獲福悟無生

The Venerable Master Hsuan Hua

His kindness and compassion cross over all; Believers are liberated and perfect the Right Enlightenment.
Transforming beings wherever he goes, his spirit remains intact;
Those who venerate him obtain blessings and awaken to the Unproduced.

WATER MIRROR REFLECTING HEAVEN

by Gold Mountain Sramana

Tripitaka Master Hsüan Hua

Preface

When the universe of a billion worlds is contemplated in stillness, one sees that bad karma has welled
up and filled it all. Nations ravage nations creating
world wars; families slay families creating civil strife;
men murder men causing wars between self and others;
people kill one another, causing war between the mind and
the nature, and so forth, until space battles space, and
water fights water, creating wars between form and the
formless. There are so many wars! How sorrowful, how
painful! Every single disaster comes from acts of destruction.

If we do not wake up soon and renounce the causes,
conditions, methods, and activities of destruction, it
will certainly be difficult to avert great disasters and
to obtain peace and happiness.

Disasters are produced from acts of destruction;
acts of destruction are produced from the mind. If the
mind does not give rise to thoughts of killing, stealing,
sexual misconduct, false speech and taking intoxicants,
if these five precepts are sternly maintained, if the
triple study (of morality, concentration, and wisdom)
is cultivated energetically, then it is certain that all
bad karma can be erased. The original face will not be
at all difficult to recognize, and it is certain that

-1-

the inherent wisdom will spontaneously appear. The scenery of the original ground has a special and wonderfully delightful flavor that is quite inexhaustible. If we wish to try its taste we must simply purify our minds.

With great heroism let us direct our thoughts toward the good; resolve to cultivate and realize the results of the Way; take others across and reach the other shore together; join the assembly of all superior and good people in one place; and forever be companions of irreversible Bodhisattvas.

This is the very purpose for which my book, WATER AND MIRROR REFLECTIONS ON AVERTING CALAMITIES, has been written. The purpose is easy to discuss but very difficult to achieve. Why is that? Consider the question of good done by living creatures. If you grab them by the ear, admonish them three times, and teach them five times, they still do not alter their conduct, yet if they encounter bad ways they advance without faltering and learn without any need for instruction. Those who understand that they should turn away from the path of confusion are few indeed.

Like the moon reflected in water, like flowers in a mirror, all these things are merely images without any substance. It may be said to be hoping for that which is without hope, accomplishing what cannot be accomplished, so it is for this reason the book is called WATER AND MIRROR REFLECTING HEAVEN.

TODAY

What is the present time? It is a time of the imminent extinction of living things. As we look around the Dharma Realm we see that countries battle each other, families contend with each other, individuals struggle against one another, on and on until great wars between world systems arise. An ancient author said, "War results from quarrels over land, and corpses fill the fields. War arises from conflicts over cities, and corpses fill the streets. The earth is made to eat the flesh of men. Such offenses are not expiated by death."

I deeply hope that the leaders of all nations will embody the preference heaven and earth have for life; establish good government and dispense justice; banish quarrelling and dispense with greed; ignore themselves and help others; benefit themselves by benefitting others; see the universe as one family and see all people as one person. A worthy one of old said, "If anyone is killed, it is as if I killed him myself. If anyone has been cheated, it is as if I cheated him myself." AT all times, look within. "If you offend before heaven, you have no place to pray."

YESTERDAY

At the age of fifty one can know the errors of the previous forty-nine years. This is not far from being a "superior man who changes his ways and moves towards the good." An author in ancient times said, "I know that my past faults were left uncorrected, yet I know that in the future I may mend my ways. I know that I

have not gone too far down the path of confusion,
and I am aware of today's rights and yesterday's wrongs."

In Buddhism it is said, "Of all bad karma which I
have done based on beginningless greed, hatred and stupidity, committed by body, mouth and mind, I now repent
and reform. Offenses arise from the mind; use the mind
to repent. When the mind is forgotten, offenses are no
more. Mind forgotten and offenses eradicated, both are
empty. This is called true repentance and reform."

It is my hope that living beings of the Dharma
Realm will read this, carefully sample its flavor, and
put it into actual practice. It is my hope that they
will deeply bring forth a sense of repentance and reform.
Confucious said, "To have faults and not change is indeed a fault... When you have faults, do not shrink
from change." There is no greater good than this.

TOMORROW

Since we have been born in this age, we must resolve to be new and great people. The engraving on the
bathtub of Emperor T'ang said, "If you can renew yourself once, renew yourself day after day; become new
again and again." The announcement to K'ang says, "Make
a new people."

Look at modern science: military weapons are modernized every day and are more novel every month. Although we
call this progress, it is nothing more than progressive
cruelty. Science takes human life as an experiment, as
child's play. It fulfills its selfish desires through
force and oppression.

Why shouldn't we think instead of washing clean the
body and mind; of brushing away accumulated dirt; of
developing a sense of shame; of painfully changing our

former wrongs to create a new life; of being unique and awesome people full of vitality; of doing beneficial deeds for the sake of all living beings in the Dharma Realm; of establishing virtue on behalf of our fellow citizens of the myriad nations; of establishing a model for all under heaven? Doing this is called representing heaven in proclaiming and teaching with kindness; and for the sake of the country, instructing the people with loyalty and filial piety.

Commentary:

Establish Good Governments

King Wen of the ancient House of Chou had such a government. He regarded the common citizens of the state as his own sons and daughters and it was his constant concern to provide for their well being. Such a leader differs from those of this age. Today there are heads of state who regard human life as a tool for the achievement of their own personal wiles or goals of the state, slaughtering, imprisoning and oppressing the people. But King Wen, while paternalistic, was not partial; he was just. Even in his time there were jails, but they were not like those of the present age with high walls of stone and steel. There is a saying, "King Wen drew the earth and made jails." If one had violated a law the King had a square drawn on the earth within which the prisoner was confined. No one thus imprisoned would leave until his sentence expired, because King Wen was not only fair but wise. He was a diviner of no small accomplishment and always knew the whereabouts of his citizens. Hence, he would tell his subjects not to move and, like obedient children, they were still. In such a way is good government established and justice dispensed.

Dispense with Greed

King Wen was first vassal to King Chou of the House of Yin. Although he was a feudal lord, the territories of King Wen covered two-thirds of the empire. Nonetheless he had not thought to displace his rightful sovereign.

Benefit Oneself in Benefitting Others

In the BOOK OF SONGS it says of King Wen:

> He measured out his magic tower,
>   measured it and planned it;
> The people built it in one day,
>   in just one day they made it.
> He measured out and built the tower,
>   he said to them, "No rush."
> And the people flocked like children.

The King is in his magic garden;
The does and bucks lie all about,
The sleek does and the white birds glisten.
The King is by the magic pond--
Ah! The leaping of the fishes.

The King made a magic garden, a spirit tower for
himself and all the people. For the benefit of all,
they willingly made it in a day.
On the other hand, an ancient ruler who is an
example of someone who exclusively engaged in vile deeds
is King Chou of Yin, the last ruler of that dynasty.
Wicked and debauched, he was under the sway of one of
his wives, Su Ta-chi, who had been possessed by the
spirit of a fox. Of all the spirits who possess people,
the fox spirit is most fierce. The fox essence is
crafty, cunning, and cruel.
Su Ta-chi disliked the King's uncle, Pi Kan, who
was a truly accomplished sage. Pi Kan was not only wise
and learned, but possessed great virtue. It was just
this virtue which frightened the fox spirit to plot his
death. Pi Kan had served the empire well, and the common people revered and honored him. His popular support
was such that to order his death would have outraged
the people. The fox spirit nonetheless was determined.
Knowing her husband, the King, to be a pragmatic man
willing to experiment, she drew on popular knowledge
and said, "Pi Kan is very clever and must be a sage.
Certainly his heart has three hairs and seven holes."
(In the heart of ordinary man there is one hair and one
hole. When the hair moves it touches the hole and knowledge arises. It is the virtue of three hairs and seven
holes that made the prime minister so wise.)
Not knowing whether his wife spoke truly or not,
the King called his uncle and said, "You really are extremely clever, certainly your heart differs from that
of ordinary men. Please lend it for inspection." Although Pi Kan was the King's uncle, he was still his
subject and so could not refuse. Obediently he opened
his chest, removed his heart, and gave it to the King.
Although he had no heart, he did not immediately
die. At that time he recalled a letter which had been
left with him by his friend, the great official and
diviner Chiang T'ai Kung, with the instructions that it
be opened only in the case of extreme danger to his life.
Feeling that the time was indeed appropriate, he read
the letter which said, "When your heart has been taken
by the King, mount a horse and ride to the north gate.
There you will find a seller of 'empty heart vegetable,
(a hollow vegetable like a green pepper). Say to him,
'Sir, if vegetables have no heart they can live. If man

-7-

has none, can he?' If that vegetable vender tells you
that man can live without a heart, you will go well. If
not, you will die."

Pi Kan mounted his horse and rushed to the north
gate where he encountered a greengrocer. "Old man," he
said, "peppers can live without a heart. Can man?"

"Of course not," came the reply. Thereupon Pi Kan,
the good minister of Yin, fell dead. His heart, inci-
dentally, was just as Su Ta-chi said it would be, with
three hairs and seven holes.

So impressed was the King with Su Ta-chi that he
gave her the title of Wise Wife and fell even more under
her influence. One day they were travelling and saw a
pregnant woman.

"She is carrying a son," said Su Ta-chi.

"How do you know?" asked the King.

"Never mind that," she said, "If you don't trust
me, just look for yourself."

"Very well," said the last King of Yin, and summoned
the woman, opening her belly with a sword to reveal the
son. The corpses of both mother and child were tossed
at the side of the road while the Wise Wife, the fox
spirit, placed her husband even more under her spell.

It is also related in the BOOK OF HISTORY how the
King and his wife stood on the balcony in the early
spring watching two men working in the thawing waters.
One, an old man, worked constantly and energetically,
unaware of the cold. The other, a young lad, shivered
in the icy waters.

"Strange," remarked King Chou.

"Not at all," said the Wise Wife. "The old man
was conceived in his parents' youth when the vital principles were in full strength. Consequently his bones
are full of marrow. That young one, on the other hand,
was conceived in his parents' last years, when they were
weak. His bones are almost empty."

King Chou scoffed.

"Take a look," she said with the air of a petulant
woman. The King summoned the two workers and sliced the
shin of each. True enough, the bone of the old man was
full, and that of the young one was like a reed, almost
empty.

Such was the conduct of the last King of the House
of Yin who took the lives of the people to be his own
playthings. It is just this disregard for the people,
committing atrocities and offenses before heaven, which
is the ruin of empires, the fall of nations, and the
undoing of kings. Such a monarch is unfit to hold the
mandate of heaven, and his past offenses persist in
spite of death. It was in the face of such wrong-doing
that the mandate of heaven ended for the House of Yin

and revolved to the House of Chou. The founder of that
dynasty was a model for the rulers of all countries, for
the good prince is truly one who turns back the light
and inspects himself, who puts forth good government and
dispenses justice, and for whom the people will come
joyfully like children and in a single day build a magic
tower.

* * *

AN AUTHOR IN ANCIENT TIMES SAID, "I KNOW THAT MY
PAST FAULTS WERE LEFT UNCORRECTED, YET I KNOW THAT IN
THE FUTURE I MAY MEND MY WAYS. I KNOW THAT I HAVE NOT
BEEN OFF THE PATH OF CONFUSION FOR VERY LONG, AND I AM
AWARE OF TODAY'S RIGHTS AND YESTERDAY'S WRONGS." These
lines are from T'ao Yuan Ming's prose poem, RETURN.
T'ao Yuan Ming, or T'ao K'an, was a recluse who once
obtained an official post in a nearby district. His
salary was a good one, consisting of five pecks of rice
a month, and his work was minimal. A month had passed
in his new post when the time came for an official
inspection. T'ao K'an, on realizing that he would have
to ride out to the boundary of his district, and there
kneel to greet the inspector, said, "I will not bend my
waist for five pecks of rice." He gave up his position
and returned to his cottage to cultivate chrysanthemums
and write.

* * *

"OF ALL BAD KARMA WHICH I HAVE DONE BASED ON BE-
GINNINGLESS GREED, HATRED AND STUPIDITY, COMMITTED BY
BODY, MOUTH AND MIND, I NOW REPENT AND REFORM." Greed,
hatred and delusion are found at the root of our actions
even those which seem to be motivated by selflessness,
love and knowledge. Difficult to understand as this at
first seems, it will be born out by sufficient inspection.

The body, mouth and mind are the vehicles which
perform the actions motivated by the three poisons:
greed, hatred and delusion. The body is capable of
killing, stealing and sexual misconduct. The mouth
spews forth false speech, confused prattle, harsh speech,
and slander. The mind governs body and mouth through
greed, hatred and wrong views. These are called the
ten paths of unwholesome conduct, and they constitute
the greater part of our conduct. However, they can be
transformed into their opposites by our efforts; this
is called turning towards the good. To change is simply
to repent. Repentance is no emotional outpouring, no
futile regret over spilt milk. We regret, and we change
and that is all there is to it. One gradually learns to

"I know that my past faults were left
   uncorrected,
Yet I know that in the future I may mend
   my ways.
I know that I have not been off the path of
   confusion for very long,
And I am aware of today's rights and yesterday's wrongs."

stop doing all manner of bad and move towards all manner
of good. This is the conduct of the superior person.
It is very simply the way by which one begins to leave
the confused and troubled state of an ordinary mortal
to become a Buddha. It must be done not merely with
words and superficial conduct but in the very depths of
the mind and consciousness. Therefore, once we begin
to put our daily lives in order, we find it necessary
to seek out a good advisor. He remonstrates with us and
teaches us the proper means of cultivation, and thus we
eliminate the accumulated garbage in our minds, stop the
deeply ingrained habits which continue to produce ever
more garbage, and attain true freedom.
"OFFENSES ARISE FROM THE MIND; USE THE MIND TO RE-
PENT. WHEN THE MIND IS FORGOTTEN, OFFENSES ARE NO MORE.
MIND FORGOTTEN AND OFFENSES ERADICATED, BOTH ARE EMPTY.
THIS IS CALLED TRUE REPENTANCE AND REFORM." The acts
of the mind are greed, hatred, and stupidity. The mind
wanders and reels about the universe of its own thought,
planning, scheming, measuring and calculating. Like a
monkey loosed in a grove of ripe fruit trees the mind
clambers on everything grasping, pulling and making a
general mess. This mad mind directs our daily activities of body and speech, hence all our offenses are
ultimately derived from the mind. Everything, in fact,
that has name and form, that is labelled and known as
distinct from other things, is a product of the mind.
We must cut off offenses at the root. Thus, what
we must reform is not merely our behavior but the very
depths of our minds. We must take our petty realms of
consciousness and expand them until we are capable of
the great conduct of the superior person, capable of
including all good deeds as well as bad ones. Reform
is in the mind, not in the shallow surface layers of
what we know as the thinking mind, but in the deep, hidden wellsprings of consciousness which can only be
reached through great effort. When we reach such depths
we pass well beyond the limitations of thinking and
verbal constructs. This is what is meant by "MIND
FORGOTTEN." It is important to understand that this
does not imply a simple forgetfulness of our wrong deeds
Rather it is a total passage beyond all normal thought,
through which we reach the very source, and there wash
off the accumulated dust.
There are, ultimately, very few who need not listen
to the words of the text, for, as it is said:

The sagely man has few errors;
The superior man changes his errors;
The petty man covers over errors;
The stupid man sees no errors.

* * *

MILITARY WEAPONS ARE MODERNIZED EVERY DAY AND MORE
NOVEL EVERY MONTH. Wars began when one person hit
another with his hand. Although it was not comfortable
for either party, the general agreement was that it was
a definitive way to deal with problems. The first
weapons were bodies which belong to the element earth.

Later, a combatant picked up a stick and found that
by wielding it skillfully, he could remain out of reach
of his opponent, yet still inflict harm on him. With
the invention of the club, the age of earth came to an
end and the age of wood began. This is simply in line
with the sequence of the elemental action. Each of the
five elemental actors produces another, which in its
turn is overcome by yet a different element. Wood is
victorious over earth. The successive action of the
elements may be arranged like this:

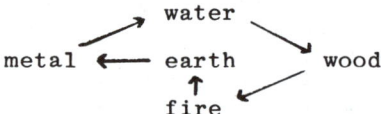

(arrows show cycle of production of elements)

Each element produces the one following it in a clock-
wise order, and is victorious over the next one in
sequence. Thus earth produces metal and overcomes water,
metal produces water and overcomes wood, water produces
wood and overcomes fire, and so forth. This production
and vanquishing of the five elemental actors is corre-
lated to the changes of the seasons, to colors, compass
points, and many other phenomena. From its profound
study, we can understand many otherwise insoluble problems of nature and history.

So it was that metal was found to be malleable and
an excellent substance for blades which could be fixed
to wooden lances and thrown from afar. Warfare continued to evolve under the influence of metal. The limits
of that element were reached when men totally encased
themselves in armor so as to be protected from arrows
and spears.

Next in line is fire. Fire overcomes metal. Gunpowder, which had existed as a plaything for years, was
harnassed and made to send pellets of metal at great
speed through the air to penetrate the suits of protec-
tive armor. Thus it came to pass that warfare raged
under the influence of fire.

It seemed as though the end of military progress
had been reached until the element water began its
ascent. Fire is overcome by water, and thus the influence of water has grown ever heavier, and under it new
weapons have emerged. The science of chemistry is under
the dominion of water, and atomic energy, which utilizes
water, is an outgrowth of chemical transformation. The
influence of fire in warfare is still paramount, but
that of water grows. As this happens what can be done?
    If we add load after load of earth to a pool of
water, we will make mud. Add more earth and we shall
finally arrive at level and dry ground, soil in which
we may plant and harvest, on which we may build. How
do we accomplish this? We use what belongs to earth,
use our bodies. With the body we can cultivate the
ground, and step by step overcome the age of water and
create dry land.
    The Buddhadharma is of the earth. It is here,
among living creatures in the world, that Dharma is
taught and practiced, not elsewhere in some starry ab-
stract heaven. Dharma is taught according to the needs
of beings. Since we are here, Dharma appears here as
it does. To the inhabitants of heavens, it appears in
an appropriate form.
    Now we are on the earth. Buddhism is of the earth,
which is why it is represented by a tawny color, the
color of earth. The Sixth Patriarch said,

    The Buddhadharma is here in the world;
    Enlightenment is not apart from the world.
    To search for Bodhi apart from the world
    Is like looking for a hare with horns.

The earth can be used for fighting, but it can also be
used to cultivate.
    The above paragraphs dealt with the defeat of the
elements by one another; the order of their production
also has great meaning for society. Yellow earth produces metal, whose color is white. On the surface of a
metal mirror one may condense water, which in depth is
black. Water nourishes and produces green wood, which
when dry, puts forth crimson flames. Fires bakes blocks
of clay into a new, durable, and useful kind of earth.
    In the earth of Buddhadharma is forged a Vajra body
like metal but stronger. With the perfection of the
Vajra body, the great depths of the waters of compassion
may be fathomed. These waters nourish the tree of Bodhi
which grows and flourishes to bear its fruit and flowers
Its wood is able to support the heat of samadhi which
fires the molded earth, burning out all impurity, and
producing a pure and durable building material.

THE GREAT MASTER CH'ANG JEN
(Filial Son Wang)

The Great Master was a native of Cheng Huang Ch'i Szu Village, Shuang Ch'eng (Twin Cities) County, in the province of Chi Lin (Lucky Grove). He was born during the later years of the Ch'ing Dynasty. He had no schooling, yet was unusually gifted and his nature was simple and honest. At the age of eighteen he heard of Yang Yi's practice of filial piety by living in a thatched hut by his parents' grave, which moved the Master to bow to his parents every morning and evening.

The great master worked and gave his money to his father who was an opium addict. When his father smoked, the Master personally stood by to serve him. His attendance was not the least remiss and yet his father continued his addiction. He would smoke and then doze off for an unfixed period of time. The Master would always wait for his father to come out of his stupor and fall into a natural sleep before going to bed himself.

One day his father awoke and felt a great sense of shame. He said, "I smoke and then sleep while you wait upon me unable to go to bed. What is more, you work during the day. This has been going on far too long and it will certainly harm you. I now firmly resolve to give up opium smoking."

The Master replied, "Please do not do so; although I have no ability I am able to work hard and provide for the necessary smoking expenses."

"Your filial thoughts are very good," said his father, "but I cannot bear to see you undergoing so much suffering. If you do not accord with my wish to stop smoking you are no longer my son." The Master did not dare reprove him further.

His father was an opium addict...
The Master would always wait for his father
to come out of his stupor and fall into a
natural sleep before going to bed himself.

Commentary:

Had the Master tried to talk his father out of his habit, there might well have occurred an emotional scene and the father, in his anger, might have only become more set in his ways out of spite for his son's impertinence. Instead, the Master merely showed his own behavior in a faithful and filial way. When his father smoked, he stood to one side watching to respond to the old man's slightest wish. When the father "nodded out" for periods of a few minutes to several hours, the son remained standing, awaiting permission to retire. Many were the times when he would stand all night only to be relieved in time to go to work in the fields. Not once did he complain during this time. His own silent example of patience and faithful service had no visible effect in a day or two, but taken together over a long period, it moved his father as nothing else could have done.

Such filial conduct can truly be called "great," since it is based on the great model of heaven and earth. Heaven and earth produce and nourish all living things and stand quietly waiting, and through their silent patience all great things come about. Slowly and silently pebbles accumulate; the vast weight and power of a huge mountain range appears. Great strength and powerful influence come, not through brief flurries of activity, but through constant perseverance.

* * *

Text:

When the Master was twenty-eight years old his parents died within a month of one another. After their burial the Master spent the days working under the blazing sun, and the nights by their graves under the open sky. After several weeks his friends and relatives in the area came to know of this and gathered their resources together to build him a hut to stave off the wind and rain. They made no windows or doors, but just used planks to block the holes.

One evening two wolves suddenly appeared, pushed down the door and jumped in. The Master was quite frightened and wished to escape, but there was no way out. He had no way to repel them and so shut his eyes and waited to be eaten while his agitated heart jumped about like a rabbit.

He thought to himself, "I am watching over these graves for the sake of my parents and if I were to be eaten by wolves while doing this I would earn a glorious death."

At that time the wolves began to close in on him, one in front and one behind. They put their forepaws up on the Master's shoulders and kept sniffing at him. The Master then put down his body and mind, collected his thoughts and contemplated emptiness. He penetrated the understanding of everything as being impermanent and devoid of a self. He silently recited the holy name Namo Amitabha Buddha without pause.. He did not know how much time passed, but the wolves finally moved, withdrew, and left, without harming a hair of the Master.

The Master was surprised by this and thought that his protection must have come about as a response from Buddhas and Bodhisattvas who secretly aided him as he was mindful--otherwise how could he still have been alive? After this he was mindful of the Buddha and recited Sutras every day with great vigor.

Commentary:

Recitation is the central practice of the Pure Land Dharma-door. "Namo Amita Buddha." "Namo" means to return in reliance, to take refuge. "Amita" means "limitless," and refers to the fact that this Buddha has both "Limitless Light" (Amitābha) and "Limitless Life" (Amitāyus). "Buddha" means "Enlightened One." So "Namo Amita Buddha" means "Homage, I take refuge in and return my life in Worship to the Buddha of Limitless Light and Life." The constant repetition of this Buddha's name is the core of the Pure Land Dharma-door.

The Buddha's teachings are taught in Five Schools: the Teaching School; the Vinaya School; the Ch'an School; the Secret School; and the Pure Land School. There are many who like to say that these are five sects, or types of Buddhism, which leads to all kinds of doctrinal

squabbling. This is not accurate; the Schools might
better be called five basic approaches to cultivation.
Each of these Dharma-doors has special appeal to certain types of people, but only one can be said to be
equally easy for all to cultivate, and that is the Pure
Land Door.

The Cultivation of the Teaching School, while serving as an excellent cure for the disease of stupidity,
does demand certain qualifications. It cannot, for example, be cultivated by the illiterate, by those who do
not know the languages in which the teachings are written, or by the very stupid. And so, although the teachings are universal, and there is not a single being who
cannot benefit from them, in their literary form there
is a definite group of people to whom they are best
suited.

The Vinaya, or "Rules and Regulations" School, requires not only that one be literate, but also that one
be living a monastic life. There is no way for the
worldly man to perfect cultivation of the Vinaya. Pure
maintenance of this Dharma-door serves as a supremely
efficacious cure for greed, desire, and arrogance. Much
of it, however, can be practiced by men and women in the
world, and can be an immense help in cultivation. All
real practicers of Buddhadharma, Sangha or lay people,
formally maintain precepts ranging from the five for
lay people through the more than 300 for bhikshunis.
There are few more awesome people in the world than the
masters of Vinaya, perfect in the 3,000 rules of deportment.

The Ch'an, or Dhyana School, stresses the practice
of meditation, and its cultivation requires a special
set of circumstances. First, it is essential to have an
advisor, one of great wisdom and skill, who can teach
the student by all manner of expedient means. Without
such a teacher, there is no way for ordinary people to
have any success in Ch'an meditation. They may achieve
some measure of attainment, but due to lack of wise
counsel, they will be turned by their experience; thinking that they are like the great Ch'an masters of old,
they will go around committing all sorts of stupid and
even dangerous or immoral acts. Such enlightened "masters" and "patriarchs" are too often well-meaning practicers of Ch'an who have either not met or not submitted
to the teaching of a good advisor. Too many of them
have entered into the various demon states that the
Buddha discussed in the SHURANGAMA SUTRA. Anyone who
professes to be a follower of the Buddha should act in
accord with his teachings and find a capable advisor,
one whose experience and lineage are unquestioned.

In addition to the above qualifications, Ch'an cultivation requires a certain temperament which is rarely

found. While some immediately find response in Ch'an
cultivation, there are many for whom it represents unbearable difficulty. If this is the only means of cultivation presented to them, many people will flee from
the Buddhadharma as a small child screams on seeing a
tamed and domesticated but incredibly fierce-looking
tiger on a leash.

The Secret School requires among other things both
a good memory to hold its many mantras and dharanis,
plus a good deal of money to carry out its elaborate
and splendid rituals. A fully adorned temple and Bodhimanda are required as well as a profusion of images
and various Dharma instruments. Also essential are numbers of Dharma Masters well trained and conversant with
the esoteric lore of this School. These are hard to
find. Without them, and without special instruction,
it is not possible to perfect the teachings of the
Secret School.

The Pure Land Dharma-door requires no great learn-
ing. Many illiterates attain inconceivable spiritual
benefit through it. Many, too, are the high and learned
masters who praise this door. The Pure Land Dharma-door
shows us how to purify our minds and as such it is
identical with the Teaching School, whose complex and
learned systems serve to keep the mind from wandering
off on useless excursions. To be able to hold the elaborate systems of the Teaching School requires prolonged
concentration on the Buddhadharma. Concentrating on
what is pure is fundamentally identical with recollec-
tion of the Buddha. The Pure Land Dharma does not require that one lead a monastic life and perfect the
three thousand awesome conducts; this Dharma-door can be
cultivated right in the midst of the most ordinary life.
Laymen and Vinaya specialists alike can cultivate this
Dharma. Nor does it require elaborate ritual and expensive ceremony, or secret esoteric lore to be learned
from specialized teachers. The secret of the Pure Land
School, and there is indeed a great secret to it, lies
in the response. It is a secret clothed not in elaborate ritual and ceremony but in the simpleness of faith
and sincerity. Its secret, which is right out in the
open, is in fact the highest secret.

The cultivation of the Pure Land Dharma-door not
only is not different from Ch'an meditation, it is Ch'an
meditation. One of the most common topics of Ch'an
meditation is "Who is mindful of the Buddha?". Investi-
gation of this topic presupposes some degree of mindfulness of the Buddha. Those who call themselves followers
of the Ch'an School and say that the Pure Land School is
a pastime for old women and stupid people, slander the
Dharma and are nothing more than those demons who Shak-

yamuni Buddha said would appear in the Dharma Ending
Age wearing the Buddha's clothing, eating his food, and
defecating in his bowl. Such so-called disciples of the
Ch'an School ignore the fact that not a single Ch'an
Master in a thousand years of history has condemned the
Pure Land Dharma as a futile exercise.

"Well," some will object, "our aim in cultivation
is to see the nature and become Buddhas instantly. This
is a secret transmission outside the scriptures and does
not rely on language. For you to sit there muttering
'Namo Amita Buddha' all day long in hope of going to
the West later on is just plain silly. No, that's
too much to take on just faith alone. I want results
and I want them now!"

The aim of all cultivation is to see the nature and become a Buddha; anything else is a waste of time and
effort. Therefore the Buddha said, "If a Bodhisattva
wishes to obtain the Pure Land he should purify his mind.
As the mind is pure, the Buddhaland is pure." To see
the Buddha of the self-nature is to see Amitabha Buddha;
to see Amitabha Buddha anywhere but in our own self-
nature is a falsehood. This is not to say that the Pure
Land in the West is merely an analogy and that there
does not exist such a place. Purify the mind in the
East and we will see the Buddhaland of the West. In
fact, purify our minds here in the East and the Pure
Land of the West will move here.

For the cultivator of Ch'an who has opened great
enlightenment, which is the goal of all cultivation,
what obstacle is there to mindfulness of the Buddha?
"In one truth," said the Great Master, the Sixth Patriarch, "is all truth; in one reality, all is real."
In keeping with the Master's teaching there can be no
obstacle to mindfulness of the Buddha, for that is just
Ch'an samadhi. Those Ch'an cultivators who are not yet
enlightened and for whom the goal seems so far off can,
by mindfulness of the Buddha, purify the Buddhaland.
This is its core. Those who would refute it are ignor-
ant of the true virtues of dhyana meditation.

The Sixth Patriarch left us these instructions:

> If drilling wood can spin smoke
>   into fire,
> A red-petalled lotus can surely
>   spring from the mud.
> Good medicine is bitter to the taste.
> Words hard against the ear
>   must be good advice.

TEXT:

One day the Master's wife came and demanded that he either return home or get a divorce; the Master did not reply. Not long afterwards she returned with her lover and, right before the Master, made a show of their intimacy. The Master remained unmoved and at peace. Thereupon, his wife and her lover left together and did not return to disturb his filial practice.

In the village there was a beancurd maker named *Meng, who was an industrious farmer. When he heard of the Master's reputation he was moved to become his Dharma protector and make offerings of food and drink. Through wind and rain he never failed in this. Three years passed in the blink of an eye and the Master resolved to stop speaking and to abstain from cooked food.

Every day he would mix raw rice flour with cold water to cure his hunger and thirst. He always sat and did not lie down. He cultivated the Vajra Samadhi and indestructible Dharma body so that a light ease often manifested and a wonderful concentration often arose. The turning wheel of cause and effect became as clear to him as the palm of his hand.

* * *

One of the Master's nieces had decided to leave home and become a bhikshuni, but the family would not

---

*Meng (孟), the beancurd maker, supported some ten people by his own labor in the fields and by selling beancurd. Beancurd, one of the staples of the Chinese diet, is so cheap that its manufacture is an affair of the very poor. In fact, it is not much above being unemployed. Meng, who figures in several incidents further on, later left home with Master Ch'an Jen who took him, not as a disciple, but as a Dharma brother with the name of Ch'ang Chih (常智). He, too, achieved great heights of cultivation.
The traditional period of mourning is three years, but since the Master was mourning both parents, he vowed to remain in the graveyard for another three years.

allow it. She said that she would ask the Master and abide by his decision. By that time, however, he had already stopped speaking and so he did not reply to her at all. After some time she left and stopped bothering him.

In meditation the Master saw his sister, Mrs. Shang, who had just decided to commit suicide because of some family problems. He then gave some simple written instructions to the Old Cultivator Meng, telling her not to kill herself. Meng went to the home of the Shang family. There he found the sister before a mirror where she was combing her hair, weeping, and crying sorrowfully. Meng said, "Your older brother is aware that you have been mistreated and sent me to talk to you. Don't act on a fit of temper; to do so would be a mistake which would later bring endless regret." Mrs. Shang was at first startled but then rejoiced and obtained a new hope in life.

One day the Master's nephew, Wang K'e Ch'in, was carried off by a group of bandits whose aim was not to rob his money but to kill him to settle a grievance. The Master, in samadhi, used the power of his Wonderful Contemplative Wisdom and saw this matter.

When the bandits drew their guns the Master used the wonderful power of spiritual penetrations to make the guns fall to the ground. The nephew managed to escape and leave no tracks.

---

*It must be clear that the Master was several miles from the scene of the kidnapping which was not as simple an affair as it might seem on first glance. It is often the case that human beings are moved to certain actions by powers outside them. The most common of these forces are various ghosts seeking release from some form of bondage. In this case, a ghost who wished to be liberated from his unfortunate state, moved a band of thugs to do his dirty work.

Such ghosts may be settling personal debts against a particular individual, but more often they may be merely trying to find anyone to take over the position they occupy, thus freeing them to

And yet, imperceptibly, there still remained a vengeful ghost who had not yet settled his accounts and who was unable to stop seeking revenge even though he knew that he was being obstructed by the Master. The ghost then sought out the Master's second younger brother and possessed his body. The possessed brother approached the grave with a knife in hand and shouted, "Filial Son Wang, you were able to save your nephew but now I will kill your brother to make good the debt!" After saying this he stood poised as if to stab himself, but the knife rose into the air and would not fall. The Master did not move a hair but sat cross-legged silently reciting the VAJRA PRAJNA PARAMITA SUTRA. He and the ghost kept at each other for a long while.

Just then, Old Cultivator Meng's heart began to pound and his skin started to crawl. He became very ill at ease and thought that perhaps something was happening at Filial Son Wang's graveyard. He ran there and on beholding this strange sight snatched the knife and thereby released the bond of hatred. Then they crossed over the revengeful ghost.

* * *

The Master continued his practice of filial piety by the graves for another three years during which time

---

(cont.) move on. When a person meets an untimely or unexpected death, his consciousness may linger on in the form of a ghost bound to the spot where the body died. Such ghosts may not travel more than several hundred feet from the spot of their death unless they can find someone to replace them. Thus it is that even today along our streets and highways there are "death rows". Such strips are simply the manifestation of successive inheritors of ghosts in a certain place luring others into their positions.

A highly efficient, if unprecedented, solution from the point of view of traffic management is to go to the places where there are ghosts, recite mantras and Sutras, and speak Dharma, thus enabling them to break their karmic bonds and go on to some other incarnation. This will break the pattern of recurrent traffic accidents.

he did not speak and ate only raw flour. At the end of this time, he sat in contemplation and tried to decide whether to go to either "Thousand Peaked" or "Wide Mountain," places where there were many old cultivating bhikshus who practiced Dhyana Meditation. Both of these were extremely still and quite places. He had decided that after his filial observances were over he would go there to practice holy conduct, leave the world, and get out of the dust. His resolve was not set on his own good alone, for he hoped to attain the great liberation and realize the fruit of enlightenment. (It is commonly said that when one son attains the Way, nine generations of ancestors escape rebirth.)

Suddenly, while in samadhi, he became aware that an honorable person would visit him the next day. Thereupon he maintained an especially sincere mind and waited. About 10:00 a.m. the next morning a poor old monk with a bindlestick came by. In his mind the Master formed the question, "Where do you come from?" The monk spoke and said, "I come from Thousand Peaked Mountain to explain some things to you and point out the road you must travel. I was an official in the Ming Dynasty. I saw through wealth and honor as if they were a spring dream and I saw power and fame as being like floating clouds. I then retired to a cave to unify my mind and regulate the will in hope of understanding the unproduced. Due to the Buddhas' compassion, although I am now over three hundred years old, I am still as strong as before and do not know old age. Your sincerity in watching over the graves of your parents and your filial conduct have moved heaven. Your virtue has transformed the multitudes. Those people with whom you have affinities are to be found in Shuang Ch'eng, not on Thousand Peaked and wide mountains.

The Master had dwelt at the grave for six years;
his ascetic practices were established and his dhyana
and samadhi were perfected. An inconceivable spiritual
state manifested, and the wonderful function of his
spiritual transformations secretly taught and saved
limitless people. Women and children received his
teaching; great officers and honorable persons took
refuge with him. His filial virtue was far reaching
and covered all classes of people. At the end of his
mourning period the fathers, elders, and brothers from
forty-eight surrounding villages joined together to hold
a ceremony of congratulations. They also made oaths
of alliance to protect the Triple Jewel and founded
Three Conditions Temple, which was to be an eternal
Bodhimanda.

* * *

In Twin Cities County, there was a family named Wu,
consisting of over eighty people living in Hou Chiu Chia
Tze (Sons of Nine Families) Village. They held a meet-
ing and decided to request the Master to go into seclu-
sion among them. They then made sincere offerings to
him and bowed respectfully.

The twenty-fifth day of the sixth month was the
festival of the Horse King God and it was a family custom of the Wu's to sacrifice a pig to obtain benefit
from the spirit. When they were about to grab the pig
it lept over a high wall and entered the room in which
the Master was secluded. It knelt before him, eyes run-
ning with tears and crying incessantly. When the Wu
family saw this strange event they could not overcome
their astonishment and exclaimed how such a thing had
never occurred before.

The Master said to the pig, "Your karma is such
that you should pay your debts. When you are released

from your present karmic retribution body I shall cross
you over so that you will be reborn among people. Do
not be confused about your earlier conditions. Cultivate pure conduct intently and when your merit is complete and the result full you will certainly realize
Bodhi and eternally be free from the suffering of the
turning wheel. You shall obtain the bliss of Nirvana.
Won't that be good?" The pig received this teaching
happily, then went to the slaughtering spot voluntarily.

Afterwards the Master called the brothers of the
Wu family together and said, "The pig which was killed
today knelt respectfully before me and begged to be
saved. Everyone in this good household must have seen
that." They replied that they had. The Master continued, "If from this day onward the entire household is
able to eat only vegetarian food and completely refrain
forever from killing I shall continue to live among you.
If you do not do this I shall go elsewhere and will not
receive the offerings of you good people again."

The elder brothers of the Wu family immediately
called a family counsel to discuss the issue. They
agreed unanimously and the entire family became vegetarians and refrained from killing, as did all their
employees and field hands. (The author personally in-
vestigated this affair in detail at the home of the Wu
family and knows it to be true.)

Influenced by this change, the inhabitants of four
nearby villages also became vegetarian and soon the custom became widespread. Those who took refuge with the
Triple Jewel numbered several tens of thousands.

* * *

It is the custom in China that during the first
month of the new year after a marriage the newly married
couple goes to the home of the wife's family to pay New

Year's respects. In accordance with this rule, Wu Kuo Chung's grandson and his bride travelled by horsecart to her family's home almost a hundred miles away for the New Year's call. Halfway along the route they suddenly saw the Great Master Ch'ang Jen seated in the cart. They asked where he wished to go and he replied, "I'm just out for a ride." I'll go along with you to the bride's family." The bride looked at him and saw that his tattered clothes and filthy face were far from elegant and asked him not to accompany them.

The Master replied, "If you don't go, I won't go; if you do, I will certainly accompany you." The couple had no recourse but to turn the cart around and return home, a few moments after which they heard that further along the road they had been travelling on were several hundred highwaymen who were holding up travelers, stealing their carriages and horses and making prisoners of the people whom they then held for ransom. The young couple then looked in the cart and found that the Master had disappeared, although they did not know when he had left.

Upon returning home the grandson questioned his granduncle, the elderly Wu Kuo Hsün, about the matter. The Elder replied, "I have been meditating with the Master and he has not gotten up from his seat for even a short time. It must have been his transformation body which rescued you. Quickly go and bow to thank him."

* * *

When the skill of one's cultivation reaches an appropriate level of attainment all sorts of states will occur as trials. Once the room in which the Master was secluded suddenly caught fire. In the same building there were over two tons of gunpowder and twenty thousand rounds of ammunition in four crates. If the flames

were to have reached this arsenal the entire family
would certainly have been destroyed. Over ten workmen
rushed in to rescue the Master and although they pulled
at him with all their strength he was like a stone image
weighing nearly a ton. It was difficult to budge him
even an inch.

Many of the little children of the Wu family saw
more than ten Filial Sons Wang on the roof putting the
fire out with water. In a short time the fire went out
by itself, much to everyone's amazement.

Afterwards the Great Master said to Wu Kuo Hsün,
"The fire was a response to something in my nature. If
the power of my samadhi had not been sufficient and if
I had been the slightest bit moved, my flesh body would
have been turned to ashes quite soon." How frightening!

* * *

At that time the Japanese had begun their invasion
the northeast provinces of China and the entire region
was in chaos. Soldiers and bandits could not be dis-
tinguished from one another as they burned, killed,
robbed and took hostages. Such activities continued
every day.

As the wealthiest family in the area, the Wus had
long been the target of thieves who, in fear that the
family would be large and well-armed, did not dare lightl
undertake to move against them. A number of bandit
groups then banded together until they were over three
thousand strong, whereupon they surrounded and attacked
the Wus. By that time the family had already moved intc
a city in Shuang Ch'eng leaving only seven persons, including caretakers and workers, at the family compound.

It looked as though it would be difficult to repel
the bandits. But the bandits, while looking at the compound from afar, saw uncountably many rifle-bearing

soldiers training their guns on them from atop the walls of the Wu household. Those who had already closed in on the compound found that they could not break in because of the strength of the doors and walls. They filled a cart with brushwood and other fuel which they then set afire against the doors. The sky suddenly clouded over and great buckets of rain extinguished the fire!

The bandits, having run out of schemes, began to upbraid one another saying, "The Wus are a great philanthropic family in this region. We should not rob them or we will incur the punishment of heaven." They then withdrew with great speed.

After this, the Master told the Wu family, "Today Kuan Kung* has made his spiritual power clear and in his protection of the good he has frightened the bandits into retreating. In the city, the clay horses in his temple are extremely tired and drip sweat as if they were being bathed with water." The next day the news arrived from the city and it was, in fact, as the Master had predicted.

* * *

Han Li Chung, also known as Shu Tung, was a nephew of the Sino-Russian War hero, Brigadier Han Kuang Ti. He had studied in Japan and on returning home had assumed the position of head of the county government. His wife had planted many good roots in past lives and believed in the proper teaching. On hearing of the Master's fame she went to pay her respects to him. Afterwards she felt the Master sitting above her head every day. When she returned to ask the causes of this phenomenon the Master replied, "In a past life you took

---

*The bandits' attack took place on Kuan Ti Bodhisattva's festival day, the 13th day of the 5th month.

refuge with me and upheld my Dharma. Because you were respectful, sincere, and earnest in making offerings to me you now have this feeling."

Mr. and Mrs. Han Li Chung heard this teaching and were extremely happy. They vowed to take refuge with the Triple Jewel and establish a temple. The construction of Three Conditions Temple depended a great deal on their work and it was with their efforts and support that it was finally completed. In accord with his own karma, the Master once developed the signs of a sickness; his entire body erupted with boils and he neither ate, spoke, nor opened his eyes for ten days. His disciples were all alarmed and frightened but their hands were tied and they had no way to help. Mr. and Mrs. Han Li Chung knelt for three days and would not stand up. For three days and nights they wept painfully and asked the Master to remain in the world rather than enter Nirvana. As a result the Master's sickness was cured without medicine.

* * *

Hsün Ch'eng Fa of Hsin Wu Village had practiced filial piety and his behavior and virtue were greatly respected by everyone. He and the Master Ch'ang Jen were fellow cultivators and were often seen together. He was known to everyone as Old Cultivator Hsün. He had a cousin named Hsün Ch'eng K'uan, who did not believe in the Buddha and whose son worked at a factory in the Japanese military complex at P'ing Fan Chan.

---

*The military camp at P'ing Fang Chan was a top-secret bacteriological and chemical warfare center. It was located next to a railyard and was so carefully guarded that passing trains were required to pull blinds across the windows when passing by. The surrounding area for several miles was closely guarded as well. Three Conditions Temple was located about half a mile from the entrance to the camp.

Once several boxes of nails were stolen from the factory, and the Japanese immediately suspected the Hsün boy of taking them. They immediately arrested both him and his father, interrogated them, and tortured them by forcing water up their nostrils; when they were full they were made to vomit. As soon as they passed out they were revived and the unendurable torture resumed.

All of a sudden, just as the torture became unbearable, they saw the Great Master Ch'ang Jen and Old Cultivator Hsün standing at their side holding beads in their hands and reciting Namo Amitabha Buddha. They soon felt no pain and were quickly released. They immediately rode in a cart to the temple and bowed their thanks. They now believed in the Buddha, took refuge, and became vegetarians. How inconceivable is the Buddhadharma!

* * *

Upasaka Li Ching Hua of Ch'ien Hsing Ling was thirty-five years old and had been married and childless for over a decade. Wishing to obtain a son he bowed to the Master with great sincerity of purpose and vowed to protect the Bodhimanda constantly with an annual offering of five tons of wheat and twenty thousand silver dollars.

The Master replied, "Your sincere resolve is good. I shall ask the Buddhas and Bodhisattvas of the ten directions to fulfill your wish. In spite of this you must still make progress in doing good and be vigorous in order to obtain spiritual protection."

Mr. and Mrs. Li asked to take refuge with the Triple Jewel and became lifelong vegetarians. Within a year they obtained an auspicious child of above average intelligence. When he was able to speak he often recited the Buddha's name and was even more fond of burning incense and bowing to the Buddha. He was especially respectful to the Sangha.

I (the author) went to the Li household many times. The child was exceptionally cordial and sincere and would always offer me food and keep me overnight. After several days I would start my travels again. This shows the strength of his good roots from past lives. In the future he will probably be a great Dharma protector.

* * *

When the Japanese invaded the three northeastern provinces and established the false puppet state of Manchuria, they set up as emperor K'ang Te, who had formerly been known as Hsuan T'ung, last emperor of the Ch'ing Dynasty. In his court there was an official named Hsi Ch'a who was plotted against and accused of disloyalty. He was taken to be tried and in his terror had decided to commit suicide. He put a gun to his head and as he was about to pull the trigger he saw an ascetic monk appear before him who said, "The charges against you will soon be dropped; don't kill yourself· for you will certainly be able to benefit the people."

When this vision had occurred three times the minister asked the Master his name and address. The Master replied that he was from Ping Fang Chan in Shuang Ch'eng County in Chi Lin Province, that he was the head of Three Conditions Temple, and that his name was Ch'ang Jen.

Shortly after this incident the suspicions against Hsi Ch'a were dropped and he was cleared of all charges. He went to Shuang Ch'eng County to investigate and found that there was, in fact, a Great Master Ch'ang Jen. He went to thank the Master personally and left the temple a plaque which read, "The Influence of Filial Piety" for a permanent momento. The number of people, military, civilian, and scholarly, who were influenced by this and who came to take refuge was uncountable.

In the twenty-eighth year of the Republic (1939) the Master went to Shang Fang Mountain near Peking to receive the transmission of Dharma from Old Master Ch'ing Ch'ih (Clear Pool).

Commentary:

Shang Fang Mountain Temple was founded by Avatamsaka Bodhisattva, whose work there disturbed the local dragons. Angry with him, they put all the water in the neighborhood into a large tank-like cart and left, thus leaving the mountain totally dry. Avatamsaka Bodhisattva then stabbed the water tank with a large spear and punctured seventy-two holes in it, from each of which water poured out and drilled into the ground. This is the origin of the seventy-two springs of S'ang Fang Mountain.

The Dharma transmission that occasioned Master Ch'ang Jen's trip to Peking was the formal transmission of the Dharma lineage. Without this transmission one cannot be an abbot or ascend the high seat.

Although the Master had built a temple and was a renowned cultivator, he still had not ascended the seat and could not do so until he had received the Dharma transmission. When he returned from Peking, so many people came to the temple that six large tents had to be erected to shelter them all. In each of these tents lectures and Dharma meetings were held. Among the visitors on that occasion was the head of the nearby Japanese military camp, who attended with a large number of officers.

Text:

When the Master returned to the temple he ascended the Dharma seat in the great hall on the seventeenth day of the third month, his birthday. On that occasion laymen gathered from more than a thousand miles around In order to extend congratulations. There were over five thousand great officials and other notables. The commander of the Japanese camp also came to pay his respects.

The areas of P'ing Fang Chan and the military camp were restricted sections through which no one was allowed to pass; on this occasion they were opened to traffic due to the enormous number of people. This was an unusual event and quite remarkable. I (the author) was present and composed the following verse of congratulations:

> Great was the filial virtue of Shǔn
>   which moved the very heavens;
> The elephants plowed his fields,
>   the birds weeded his crops.*
> The Master's filiality
>   is even greater now;
> Gods and people together rejoice, and
>   the Buddhas smile.

---

*The Emperor Shun, one of the earliest Chinese emperors, was renowned for his filial piety. His father wished to kill him and contrived all sorts of devious plans to do so, including setting his son to work in a granary which was then set aflame. Shun, two straw hats in hand, parachuted to safety from the roof. When sent to clean out a well on the family property, Shun suddenly found his younger brother dropping an enormous boulder down on him. Shun avoided drowning through the intervention of a local spirit who led him through an underground watercourse connected with the well. He emerged unharmed, unknown to his murderous father and brother, and returned to his home. Hsiang, under the impression that his brother was safely drowned at the bottom of the well, rushed home and said to his father, "Let my parents have the oxen and sheep, let them have his storehouses and granaries. I shall have his shield and spear. I shall have his lute, his bow shall be mine, my two sisters-in-law shall attend upon my couch." Hsiang rushed to his brother's house to claim his prizes and found Shun sitting calmly playing the lute. Shun the Filial, although he knew what his brother was up to, greeted him quite cordially. This quality in his character moved heaven and earth to help Shun in his daily work. When he plowed his fields wild elephants came voluntarily under yoke to draw the plow. When weeds sprouted, birds flew in from the wilds and weeded the field.

After the Master had ascended the high seat and the congratulations were over, it was decided to establish a monastery to increase the dwellings for the Sangha so that large numbers of monks from the ten directions might be accommodated. A great sum of money was required to build such a place and one wealthy merchant wished to give it all himself. The Master put him off amiably and said, "In a bodhimanda of the ten directions there must be donors from the ten directions who will give and plant blessings. Therefore, I wish to go about and beg from every dwelling. As it is said, 'Accumulated foxhair armpits make a coat,' 'A city is founded through the plans and strength of many who plant virtuous roots.'"

From thence the Master and I (the author) would go out to beg from door to door. We never overlooked the poor or lowly in favor of the rich or honored. With great kindness and equanimity, the multitudes were universally crossed over.

Commentary:

This proverb might be rendered in English as "Accumulated ermine tails make a coat." In both cases the fur in question is extremely soft, warm and beautiful yet constitutes only a small portion of a small creature. A coat made of the inch-long piece of fine pelt found in the armpit of a fox requires an enormous number of pelts. So, too, in his begging, the Master wanted to accumulate small quanitities from as many donors as possible rather than take a large amount from one person.

Text:

I (the author) recall that in Tung Ching Tzu (East Well) Village there was a family named Chang, who raised extremely fierce wolf-like dogs whom everyone feared as if they were tigers. No one would dare visit the family. But when the Master and I reached that door on our rounds the dogs behaved like lambs. Much to everyone's astonishment they wagged their tails to welcome us.

One time we reached the Wu family village on our rounds and went to the home of Wu Wen Hui. The Master and I were talking and discussed the amount we had collected. When counted it was found to be quite a large sum, and the Master felt rather proud of himself and a bit smug. He said that it had all been given because people had heard of the fame of the Filial Son Wang (he spoke of himself). He said that it was because of this that they rushed to fling money at him and that this was not occurring through the help of anyone else.

From that time onward I remained silent and did not say a single word in order to show my criticism. At eight o'clock that morning we went to solicit from over ten of the town leaders and elders as well as from a number of other honorable people. We stopped at every door until eleven o'clock, at which time we returned to the Wu house for lunch.

When the money was counted it was found to total scarcely twenty-four dollars, the smallest amount ever recorded. I laughed and said to the Master, "Now, Abbot, where has the light of the Filial Son Wang gone?"

The Master replied, "You should no longer remain silent. I know that I spoke wrongly and that in fact the donations were a result of 'borrowing your light.' I hope that you will reveal a 'vast and long tongue' and that we will work hard together.

"All right," I agreed.

* * *

There was, at that time, a carpenter named Chang to whom I said, "When our temple is being built you should help out with ten days of carpentry. How about it?" He agreed and I then asked him what his daily wage was. He replied that it was twelve dollars and I said, "It

will be enough for you to give four days' wages." He
protested that he did not have it and I said, "It's in
your pocket." Lo and behold, there were exactly forty-
eight dollars in his pocket, not a penny more or less.
The carpenter could not overcome his astonishment at
the strangeness of this matter.

* * *

In the Chinese custom, married women like to hear
auspicious talk, so many women with babies would bring
them to the Master and ask if the child would grow up
well. The Master always replied that this would be the
case. One day I asked the Master privately, "Abbot, do
you really know whether or not those children will be
easily brought up? Why do you say that they will be
easily raised?"

"I say so because their mothers like to hear such
talk," he replied.

"Once," I said, "someone asked you this question and
you answered affirmatively, yet the child died within
three days."

"What would be the perfect answer?" asked the Master.

"The next time the question is asked, have the
questioner ask me," I said.

One day someone came with a baby and asked the usual
question. I answered, "If you want to know if your
child will grow up well, you must ask yourself. If, for
example, the child should have a long life and be talen-
ted but you, his parent, were to lead a totally disso-
lute life, you might very well do deeds which would cut
off the child's life. In that case, if I were to give
an auspicious prediction it would go unrealized. If,
on the other hand, the child should have a short life
and I were to tell you so, and thereupon you were to
examine yourself constantly and do meritorious deeds,

you could increase the child's lifespan. In that case
you could accuse me of not giving an accurate prediction.
Therefore, you must look for the answer in yourself; do
not look outside."

* * *

In Harbin we once encountered a Western Catholic
priest who said, "The Buddhist practice of bowing before
images is a superstitious one. What benefits does it
bring?"

I answered, "What benefit is there in your not bowing before images?"

"We are not superstitious," he said.

"The Buddhist practice of bowing to the Buddha,"
I replied, "diminishes one's habits of self-importance,
pride, and arrogance. It is also a good physical exercise that can make the body strong. Is there anything
more beneficial than that? Besides, what you call super-
stition, or confused belief, is just an ordinary word.
The great error lies not in confused belief but in belief in the confused. Those of confused belief are common people and, although they are confused, they still
are capable of wishing to have faith in the proper Dharma and in the future they will certainly become Buddhas.
On the other hand, those who believe in the confused are
adherents of externalist paths, and although they may
believe, theirs is a case of the blind leading the blind
into an improper path. Those who are confused and un-
awakened create karma and undergo retribution which is
unspeakably bitter. They seek escape but are unable to
attain it.

"In addition to these, there are those who are confused and who do not believe. These are Heavenly Demons
who fall into the retinue of the Demon King where they
believe even less in the proper Dharma. Their sufferings

and sorrows are even more unbounded.

"In addition to the above there is a fourth kind who believe and who are not confused. These are various sages and worthies. Because of belief in the proper Dharma they obtain the result of enlightenment, the light of Prajna constantly shines and smashes the darkness of delusion and they attain the gate of the highest expedient device."

* * *

Although Hiroshima had been blasted by the atomic bomb and the Japanese had surrendered, the misfortunes of the Chinese people were not yet over. The Northeast was invaded by the Russians who stole, burned, murdered, and robbed people at road blocks. They did every kind of evil.

I was accompanying the Elder Abbot, who was returning to the temple carrying over a million dollars when we encountered a number of Russian soldiers who stopped us for inspection. There was nothing we could do to drive them off. The Abbot placed his palms together and recited the name of Ten Thousand Merits, Namo Amita Buddha, without pause; he was not even the least bit harmed by the brigands.

When we reached the temple I mentioned how the situation was chaotic and how we should stop the work of this project while waiting for a better opportunity.

The Abbot said, "No."

I replied, "I will no longer take part in this fundraising campaign."

From that time on I roamed around teaching those with whom I had an affinity. The Great Master Ch'ang Jen continued to be girt with the armor of vigor as a good field of merit for living beings. After completing the temple he went to Peking and attained Perfect Still-

If the deeds done in a hundred thousand aeons
    are not eradicated,
The retribution will be experienced
    when the conditions become ripe.

ness while seated at Nien Hua (Twirling Flower) Temple.
He was seventy-two years old and his precept age was
twenty-two.

THE INTERWOVEN NET OF KARMIC RESPONSES
OF CAUSE AND EFFECT

The Dharma Realm is not large; a mote of dust is not
small. Why? All is one and one is all. Yet there is
something more wonderful, subtle, and difficult to believe than even this: the net-like interweaving of
karmic responses, and the wheel-like spinning of cause
and effect.

For example, the karmic influences between countries
are interwoven; the causes and effects of their mutual
debts and repayments compel them to ceaseless wars. It
becomes difficult to stop the murders and massacres
which increase endlessly until the final destruction of
the countries and the annihilation of all races when
everything is eradicated and brought to an end. There
is a saying, "Plant good causes, reap good results; plant
bad causes, reap bad results." How true it is!

There is also this interweaving of karmic influences
as well as the causes and effects of mutual debts and
repayments between families. When there is kindness,
there is harmony, but when enmity arises there is revenge. The participants do not understand, and continue
to rail at each other for life. Who awakens from this?

A Sutra text says, "If the deeds done in a hundred
thousand aeons are not eradicated, the retribution will
be experienced when conditions become ripe." In all our
actions, how can we possibly not be cautious and attentive, "as if standing on the edge of a deep abyss, as
if treading on thin ice"!

To find the interwoven threads of causal relation-
ships, it is not necessary to delve into obscure and
ancient accounts. The following is an account of a well-
known event which occurred at the end of the Ch'ing
Dynasty at Tuo Huan Chan, a mere ten miles or so from my
(the author's) home in northeast China.

Among the various Chinese medicinal herbs is ginseng, a variety of mandrake, particularly valued as a
cure-all and tonic. So prized is this root for its life-
giving and revitalizing powers that the mountains of
Northern China and Korea, where the best quality root
is often found, became the home of many "prospectors"
in search of rare finds worth more than their weight in
gold.

Not only does the appearance of the ginseng plant
strangely resemble the human trunk, but it has other
human-like qualities as well. When a wild root has been
exposed to the sun and moon and the energies of other
natural forces for many years, it may manifest its own
life force and develop a certain magical intelligence.
This is true only for roots which have managed to grow
to at least a pound in weight; anything less than that
is merely extremely high-quality medicine. It takes a
minimum of three thousand years for a root to mature to
sufficient size to have such magical powers. Consequently anyone who could find such an extremely prized
root would be set up in incredible wealth for life.

In addition to their scarcity, such roots are hard
to find because they are clever enough to sense the
approach of a prospector and will immediately burrow
underground. Uncommon is the person with skill and luck
enough to trap and seize such a root before it has a
chance to flee.

During the time I'm thinking of, there were two

such ginseng prospectors who had sworn an oath of brotherhood before an image of Kuan Kung. A three-year mountain expedition had yielded little of value; their provisions were reduced to three cups of rice. Being so far in the mountains with so little food left, they were on the verge of starvation, when at last their years of wandering in those isolated regions paid off. They managed to find and trap the most incredible ginseng root ever known--one weighing a full pound and a half.

As they bound up their priceless treasure and started the long trek down the mountain, Ming Wu Yeh, the older of the partners, got so greedy thinking about what reward this root would bring when presented to the emperor that he went a little crazy. His greed took control and, unable to bear the thought of sharing this fortune with anyone, he impulsively shoved his sworn brother and fellow prospector off the edge of a sheer cliff. His young partner plummeted to his death thousands of feet below and Ming went on his merry way.

As sole possessor of this fantastic root, he still had other worries, however. There was a major border to cross and he knew the border guards were a crooked and greedy lot. If they uncovered his pound and a half ginseng root it was for sure they'd confiscate it and perhaps murder him in the process. Agitated but spurred on by his greed, Ming plotted how he could deceive the border inspectors. Finally, he decided to put the root in a coffin and nail it shut. When he passed the border he would weep and wail about the passing of his kin and beg them to let the dead rest in peace and not disturb the coffin. With the reward as incentive, he managed to put on a good show, but the guards were heartless and set about prying open the pine box.

Frozen with terror and stricken with regret that he

hadn't devised a more clever plan, the prospector stood
by holding his breath as the lid came off. Lo and behold, inside lay, not a gnarled ginseng root, but a
placid figure of an old bearded gentleman, resting light-
ly with his eyes closed. Barely able to contain a shout,
Ming helped reseal the coffin and hurried on his way.
"I've really got something here," he chuckled to himself as he set as fast a pace as he could straight for
the imperial palace.

Needless to say, the emperor graciously accepted
the gift and awarded his subject so amply that Ming was
able to purchase all the land on either side of the road
from the capital to his home, a full three hundred miles
and thus was able to "drink from his own wells" on his
travels.

The next thing he did with his vast fortune was
commission the construction of a mansion in which every
brick had four bronze coins baked into it. The pillars
rested on silver supports, and the mortar holding the
bricks together was made from silver dust. With such
an exterior, you can imagine what must have been used
to furnish and embellish the rooms and corridors of his
home. Gardens and parks adorned the estate and in these
luxurious surroundings Ming lacked nothing--except a son

But then his wife was with child again and when she
was close to term, Ming Wu Yeh was seated in a pavilion
in his courtyard when suddenly he saw the form of his
sworn brother whom he'd pushed off the cliff those many
years ago. His partner strode toward him across the
manicured lawns laughing, and then the vision disappeared, as a servant arrived with news that his wishes
had been fulfilled--he had a son. But the price had
been great, for his wife had died in childbirth.

That was not the first price this unusual child

would cost Ming. The boy's disposition was such that he
would cry incessantly until given something to play with,
whereupon he would smash the object to smithereens
amidst spasms of laughter. Eventually he developed more
and more discriminating tastes and would only be quieted
if he were given an expensive enough object to break.
As he grew into a young man his interests changed but
his insatiable insistence on being provided with money
for entertainment, gambling, fine food and all the
pleasures of life never slacked. He was totally irre-
sponsible and had no scruples whatever when it came to
squandering his father's fortune.

Helpless to stop his son's reckless behavior, Ming
grew more and more depressed as he watched his fortune
dwindle. His continual admonishments to save for the
future and perpetuate the family estate fell on deaf
ears. Finally on his death bed he admonished his son
to remember that the house itself was worth a fortune
and not to forget the wealth hidden in the walls.

Ming died and his son continued to drink and gamble
the fortune away until he became penniless with nothing
remaining but the bare walls of his father's mansion.
But rather than heed his father's last instructions, the
son recklessly sold the house to a stranger for roughly
the cost of the mere bricks.   Thus within a short
time the ill-gotten fortune was spent.

The principle of karma is vividly illustrated in
this unusual but true account. You can apply this principle to all situations that occur in the world because
karmic retribution is indeed interwoven and the net we
weave is ultimately the snare which catches us.

In flocks of good and packs of evil,
People always seek their own kind.

IDENTICAL INTEREST GROUPS

The standard phrase,

In flocks of good and packs of evil
People always seek their own kind,

sums up the concept of identical interest groups. Scholars are friendly with scholars, farmers with farmers, workers with workers, businessmen with businessmen, and officials with other officials. Buddhists are friendly with Buddhists, Taoists with Taoists, Christians with Christians, and Moslems with Moslems. Military personnel consort with military personnel, bandits with bandits, good citizens with other good citizens, and deviant people with other deviant people.

Each person seeks out his own kind, and thus parties and special interest groups are established in mutual jealousy and enmity. Such groups are as compatable as water and fire, that is, they will not tolerate one another. They start out well but gradually give rise to resentment and hatred and after a time they begin to devour one another. The strong overpower the weak and the many take advantage of the few. Strength comes to outweigh reason and thus we reach the present sorry state of affairs.

* * *

THE ENDLESS TURNING WHEEL OF KARMIC RETRIBUTION

The revolving wheel of karmic retribution turns on without cease. Sheep can become people and humans can become sheep, as explained in the SHURANGAMA SUTRA. There are nations of sheep, nations of horses, nations of cows, of pigs, of dogs and so forth down to the nations of bees, ants, mosquitoes, and other insects. Each of these gathers in groups of its own kind. The strong

-47-

become kings and the many become the nation. All of
this occurs in accord with the retributions for the deeds
done in the past, and this retribution is never off by a
hair's breadth.

Notes:

The term "nation" here may be taken in two senses.
On one hand it indicates the collectivity of any particular species such as all horses or all sheep. On the
other hand it can also refer to rebirth from one into
another species. People who are fond of mutton, for
example, establish an affinity with the nation of sheep
and are then reborn into that nation. Those who eat a
great deal of beef move into the country of cattle and
find themselves in bovine bodies. Many persons find
this principle difficult to believe. Regardless of one's
belief or disbelief, pragmatic demonstrations of this
idea inevitably occur to everyone. Simply keep doing
what you are doing, and you will sooner or later reap a
reward commensurate with your activity.

Text:

When viewed with the Buddha Eye it is all total in-
version. Suddenly beings soar to the heavens and then
plummet to the earth. Suddenly they are people, suddenly
they are ghosts, suddenly they are hell beings, suddenly
they are asuras, and then, just as suddenly, flittering,
flying, crawling, and creeping things. Beings undergo
these retributions in accord with their own past deeds
yet remain quite unaware that this is happening. How
pitiful this is. An ancient verse says,

> Just out of a horse's belly, and into a
>   donkey's womb,
> How many times have you passed by Yama's door?
> Having just gone before Lord Shakra,
> Now you end up in Yama's pot.

From this one should see the successions of lives and
deaths as being unfixed like the bobbing of motes of

dust floating in the wind of karma, sinking into the
six paths without rest.

Notes:

Yama, the Lord of the Dead, presides over the tri-
bunals in the hells. His face is as dark as iron and he
is totally devoid of human feelings. When people have
committed offenses they are sent off to hell. It is not
the case, however, that Yama, who is actually a great
Bodhisattva, orders people to go to these places intend-
ing to harm creatures, and that they follow his instructions. Nor is it the case that some god proclaims the
destinies of beings. Gods, even Buddhas themselves, are
all made from people. There is not any fixed predeter-
mination of what any being will be. People go to hell
not because Yama sends them, but because the power of
their own karma drives them there. Other people become
Buddhas not because they are inherently any more enlightened than others; it is just that they spend enormous
aeons preparing and cultivating the practices conducive
to Buddhahood.

* * *

WHAT IS THE ULTIMATE MEANING OF THE MIDDLE WAY?

"Ultimate" means final, "meaning" means what is
fitting, "middle" means not going to extremes, and "Way"
means practice. One who abides by the Middle does not
go too far, nor does he fail to go far enough. When he
goes too far he should bring about a lessening, and when
he falls short, he should increase. In either case he
should avoid falling into emptiness, or grasping at existence. This is what is meant by the Middle Way, the
true substance of the principle of True Emptiness. It
is also called the Reality-Mark, True Suchness, One's
Own Nature, and the Buddha-nature.

To put it quite clearly once again, it is like the
figure zero which is the sole ancestor of heaven and
earth, the father of all Buddhas, the mother of all
things, and the source of the most subtle of wonders.

Everything in life and death comes from it and there isn't anything which does not return to it. This is what is meant by the phrase "True Emptiness is not empty, Wonderful Existence is not existence." One who understands this can be called a "person of the Way who is without a mind," one who has overstepped all categories, who has been released forever from the suffering of the wheel, who roams freely at leisure, and who has ended birth and death--a living dead person.

* * *

PLEASURE IS THE CAUSE OF SUFFERING

The Saha World is characterized by the blaze of ten-thousand sufferings. It is full of a great many evils. There are many ways to suffer, three, eight, and a limitless number of ways, but it is difficult to discuss them; they can never be fully described. The three sufferings are

1. the suffering within suffering,
2. the suffering of deterioration, and
3. the suffering of process.

The eight sufferings are,
1. birth,
2. aging,
3. sickness, and
4. death,
5. the suffering of being separated from objects of love,
6. the suffering of encountering objects of hate,
7. the suffering of not getting what what one seeks, and
8. the suffering of the raging blaze of the five skandhas.

Wearing beautiful new clothes is a great pleasure, but before long the clothes become a yoke. When they get dirty or stained, worry arises. Would you call this pleasure or suffering?

Fine eating is foremost among pleasures, and so hundreds of delicacies have been invented. Nonetheless, a gourmand can eat only three times a day; more brings on vomiting and diarrhea. Would you call this pleasure or suffering?

Elegant estates are considered great pleasures. And yet although one may accumulate thousand of dwellings, during sleep one's realm extends less than eight feet. All those houses need stewards, and caring for them exhausts one's mental faculties. Would you call this pleasure or suffering?

* * *

A BURNING HOUSE WITHOUT PEACE

The place where we live is forever disturbed by countless terrors, miseries, and troubles. One day there are earthquakes, the next day landslides, and the next, tidal waves. All kinds of calamities follow one upon another endlessly, which is why those of old said, "The triple world knows no peace; it's like a burning house."

After he left the home life, the Great Master Lien Ch'ih often returned to visit his family. His wife, endowed with much wisdom and wholesome roots, searched for a method to help him, and came up with the following means. Just inside the door she dug a pit. In it she set live coals. When the Master set foot inside the house, he stepped into the fire and let out a great yell.

"This is a pit of fire!"

His wife replied, "Since you know it's a fiery pit, don't come back anymore." The Master then had a great awakening . Later he became an outstanding personage in Buddhism.

THE WAY OF FRATERNAL RELATIONS

During the Han Dynasty, the family of a four year-old boy named Kung Yung received a gift of a box of pears. All his brothers took large ones while Kung Yung deliberately sought out the smallest. Surprised, his elders asked the boy about his behavior.

"My brothers are older than I and they should get the big ones. Since I am the youngest it is fitting that I receive the smallest," he replied.

Although Kung Yung was young, he had a profound understanding of the principles of yielding and filial respect. More of such behavior would truly influence the world.

* * *

LOYALTY AND DUTY

We should have a sense of responsibility in everything we do. We should carry out our duties to the utmost of our ability. It is most important neither to ignore responsibility, nor to conduct affairs in a slack or partial manner, nor to be remiss in fulfilling commitments. Otherwise we will only undermine our own future and experience unbounded regret.

Those who deal loyally with others will be dealt with loyally, whereas those who deal falsely with others will be dealt with falsely. The cheater cheats himself; he who harms, harms himself. If one sends out "counterfeit money" the same returns to him. How could we be anything but careful!

THE IMPORTANCE OF FAITH

Faith is the foundation of cultivation of the Way, and the mother of merit and virtue, because it is capable of nourishing wholesome roots. The Buddhadharma is like a vast sea; only by faith can it be entered. Therefore, the single word, faith, is the essence of escape from birth and death, and is the wonderful means for returning to the source. It is a precious raft in the stream of affliction, a torch in the dark cave of ignorance, and a guide who leads us out of the path of confusion. It is a compass for those floundering in the waves on the sea of suffering, and a sagely teacher for those in the three paths and the eight difficulties. It is the origin of awakening for the four kinds of creatures born within the six paths. Faith cannot be ignored. An author of ancient times said, "If a man has no faith, I do not know what can be made of him."

Once two bhikshus were travelling to see Shakyamuni Buddha, the World Honored One. As they travelled they became extremely thirsty but could not find any water. As they walked they happened upon a human skull containing water in which some small bugs were swimming, enjoying themselves tremendously. One of the bhikshus picked up the water and offered some to his companion. The companion replied, "This water contains bugs and the precepts do not permit drinking such water. I would rather die of thirst than to violate the precepts in order to stay alive." After this incident he died of thirst.

When the bhikshu who had drunk the water reached the place where the Buddha was residing, he bowed and said to the Lord, "Your disciple was travelling in the company of another bhikshu who perished of thirst on the road. I hope the Buddha will be compassionate and rescue him."

The Buddha said to the bhikshu who had drunk the water, "Because he stringently maintained the precepts and was so firm in his faith that he would not violate them even in the face of death, he received the awesome power of the Buddhas and arrived here before you. He has already seen the Buddha and heard the Dharma before you. He is a bhikshu who has true faith in the precepts."

* * *

THE CONCEPT OF PROPRIETY

The word propriety is defined by a homonym in Chinese which means "to set up" or "to stand". Therefore, Confucious said, "If a man has no sense of propriety he has nothing to stand on." It is also said of one's parents, "Serving them with propriety while they are alive, burying them with propriety after death, and making sacrifices on their behalf with propriety is filial piety."

Confucious's disciple, Tse Hsia, asked about filial piety. The Master replied, "It consists in not getting angry."

When Tse Yu asked about filial piety the Master replied, "What people nowadays call filial piety is simply feeding the parents. But they can feed dogs and horses just as well. If there is no respect involved, how do we differ from them?"

Yen Yuan asked about humaneness and the Master replied, "It consists of subduing the self and returning to propriety." The disciple asked what was meant by subduing the self and returning to propriety and the Master replied, "Look at nothing improper, listen to nothing improper, say nothing improper, and do nothing improper."

Lord Kuan's name was Yu, and his pen name was
Yun Ch'ang. He was an outstanding personage of the late
Han and Three Kingdoms period, and the great hero of the
Western Han. His entire life was noble and marked with
an overwhelming air of righteousness which no one could
equal. He protected his imperial sister-in-law, holding
a candle until dawn to resist the opportunity for misconduct offered by a darkened room. He galloped a thousand miles in search of his brother.

Although he was granted gold and the seal of high
office, in the midst of wealth and honor he did not in-
dulge in promiscuity, nor was he moved by poverty; moreover, he did not succumb to military oppression. From
then to now there has never been anyone like him.

* * *

INCORRUPTIBILITY

In ancient times the Emperor Yao wished to abdicate,
and sought a sage to whom to yield the empire. He had
heard of the two sages Ch'ao Fu and Hsü Yu, who were
pure and lofty in their conduct, and he humbly went in
person to visit them. When he met Ch'ao Fu he explained
his intent to yield the empire to him. On hearing this,
Ch'ao Fu covered up his ears and ran off to wash them.

Hsü Yu, who happened to be downstream at the river
bank watering his ox, was surprised by this strange behavior, and inquired about it. Ch'ao Fu replied, "The
Emperor Yao just offered the empire to me. Such words
defiled my ears and so I am washing them."

Hsü Yu answered, "Washing your ears in this water
pollutes it. How can I let my ox drink such defiled
waters." Thereupon he moved his ox upstream. Ah! How
incorruptible these two were.

AFRAID LEST THEIR ACTIONS
NOT EQUAL THEIR WORDS

Pai Yi and Shu Ch'i were brothers who lived at the
time of King Chou of Yin. When King Wu of Chou arose
to avenge the people and punish the wrongdoing (of King
Chou of Yin), the two went out on horseback to remon-
strate with him and say that a subject could not punish
his sovereign and bring about confusion in the world.

King Wu replied, "King Chou is infatuated with his
concubine, T'an Chi. He has sliced open the marrow of
citizens, and ripped open the wombs of pregnant women.
His lust is unbridled and he robs and abuses the people.
He is rejected by the gods and is nothing but a merci-
less autocrat. I ride against a mere commoner. I have
to save the people who are as if trapped between water
and fire. How is this making confusion?"

After that he went on to destroy King Chou and
change the name of the Dynasty from Yin to Chou. Pai
Yi and Shu Chi were ashamed to eat the grain of the
state of Chou and retired to Shou Yang Mountain where
they starved to death. To this day they are praised
for their righteousness and sense of shame.

VIRTUE OF CHARACTER

The reason that human beings are the most magical among the ten thousand creatures is because they are aware that they can cultivate virtue of character. Therefore, one's words should be trustworthy, and one's actions must be prompted by utmost reverence. We should treat others with sincerity, teach them with earnestness, and observe the rules of courtesy with caution. Whenever things don't go our way, we should seek the problem within ourselves. We should get rid of selfish motives and embrace a public spirit. Above, we should emulate the Buddhas of the ten directions, embodying great kindness toward those with whom we have no affinities. We should universally save all living beings so they can together escape the wheel of suffering and accomplish the Buddha Way. Below we should be mindful of our kin within the three evil destinies, who are still undergoing retribution for their offenses in the unintermittent hell. Quickly we should rescue and pull out our relatives and friends, so that they all leave the realms of ghosts and hells, and together certify to Bodhi. We should always maintain this resolve, and make firm our practices and vows. If we haven't reached this goal, we vow to never rest. Hence, as a means to decisively fulfill our vows, we should proceed to establish virtue of character.

* * *

WRITTEN WHEN THE JAPANESE
WERE INVADING CHINA

With my feet astride Mount Sumeru and my head
    reaching up to the sky,
Single-mindedly I dare to switch the sun's place.
May both East and West become the Land of
    Ultimate Bliss,
And Nanching and Peiching unite.*
Let us clean up the warfare that plagues
    the universe,
And extensively bless mankind with beneficent
    government.
May all those within the Dharma Realm enjoy
    health and peace,
And together attend the celebration of Bodhi's
    fruit of enlightenment.

----

*The Southern Capital and Northern Capital of
China.

* * *

CULTIVATING THE BODHISATTVA WAY

PU SA transliterates the Sanskrit word, BODHISATTVA,
which translates as "One who enlightens sentients." This
refers to one who cultivates the different practices of
benefiting living beings, thereby enlightening oneself
and enlightening others, rescuing oneself and rescuing
others. One subjugates the self for the sake of others,
and with kindness embraces all creatures. One is proper,
public-minded, illustrious and bright. Since such a
one's every move is dedicated to rescuing living beings, he
is called "One who enlightens sentients." In bringing
forth the Bodhi resolve and practicing the Bodhisattva
path, the important thing is to be resolute and perservering,

and to remain steadfast and unchanging with regard to one's vows and resolve. Don the armor of vigor, wield the Prajna sword and slay the mad thieves of the six faculties.[1] Capture the skandha ghosts of the six consciousnesses.[2] Wipe out the defiled demons of the six dusts.[3] Diligently cultivate the Dharma field of the Six Paramitas. Irrigate the garden of the six paths. Nurture the flowers and fruits of the ten thousand conducts. Groom an indestructible Vajra body, and achieve an inconceivably splendid result. And then, upon becoming replete with the ten thousand virtues, with an efficacious light that radiates, manifest the eight marks of certifying to the Way,[4] and realize Buddhahood in a hundred realms. Only then is the work of a great person fully accomplished!

---

[1] The eyes, ears, nose, tongue, body and mind, which rob us of our inherent treasures.

[2] Seeing, hearing, smelling, tasting, touching, and knowing.

[3] The six sense objects of sights, sounds, smells, tastes, objects of touch, and dharmas .

[4] Every Buddha manifests eight marks of accomplishing the Way:
>   descending from the Tushita Heaven,
>   entering the womb,
>   dwelling in the womb,
>   leaving the womb,
>   leaving home,
>   subduing demons,
>   accomplishing Bodhi,
>   entering Nirvana.

REPAYING PARENTS' KINDNESS

As our parents' children, the very first thing we should understand is that their kindness is higher than the heavens and deeper than the sea. If we do not try to repay their kindness, then we should bring forth great shame and remorse, for we will have been people in vain. In wishing to repay this debt of kindness, foremost we must rectify our character and establish virtue, address the fundamentals and cultivate the Way. As it is said,

When one child attains the Way,
Nine generations of ancestors are
reborn in the heavens.

How can we be remiss? Another ancient adage goes,

Among the hundred good acts,
Filiality is foremost.

Those who can truly cultivate can be reckoned as being truly filial. And those who are truly filial are those who can truly repay their parents' kindness. Therefore, we should have our feet firmly planted on the ground, and advance bravely. In no circumstance should we be lazy, or try to shirk our duty and squander the time away. Otherwise, not only will it be difficult for us to repay our parents' kindness, it will also be difficult to save ourselves.

* * *

CHENG TE: A PARAGON OF FILIALITY

There was a boy named Te ("Virtue"), son of the Cheng family who lived at Wu Chang ("Five Constants") County, east of Chi Lin ("Auspicious Grove"). When he was five, by his own heavenly nature he already knew how to be filial to his parents. He would inquire about their well being in morning and evening and make sure that they were warm in winter and cool in the summer.

At daybreak and nighttime he would pay his respects to them, and moreover bow to them with utmost reverence. And he would never taste any food or drink himself until he had first offered them up to his father and mother.

By and by the virtue of his filial piety became well known near and far, and many teachers and exponents of externalist paths and deviant sects came to call at his house, wishing to recruit the boy into their camp so they could exploit him for their own advantage. Each of those teachers revealed his "three-inch long tongue" and spouted forth glib and crafty debate that flowed like an uninterrupted river. But their wild ravings failed to inspire faith in the pure youth's mind. And although their theories were as incessant and profuse as the waves of the Yangtze River, nonetheless, they could not move the sincere resolve of that young boy.

Of these teachers, some would claim, "My path is number one. In the future the ten thousand teachings will all return to this one path, and all of them will become disciples. Now that you have the opportunity to first enter upon my way, in the future you will be the elder disciple."

To this Cheng Te would reply, "Since I am still young, first I have to discharge   my filial duties and bring joy to my parents. When I grow older, I shall select a wholesome path and pursue it."

Another teacher would say, "My path is the greatest, even the Patriarchs of the Confucian School, the Buddhists and the Taoists are my sons and grandsons. You should now recognize your master and return to the founding school. That way you will be the most filial son or grandson of the Buddha."

To this Te would reply, "My thinking is still young and naive, and I am not yet qualified to walk the Great Way. This is like studying. A person would certainly

have to attend elementary school before going into a
university."

Another teacher would say, "My path is the most
fundamental. It is the mother of the ten thousand
teachings. They all return to my path, just as falling
leaves all return to the root. This teaching is the
original source of all Buddhas, and nothing lies outside
of this path of mine. You should quickly enter upon my
path."

Te would answer, "What I consider as fundamental is
somewhat different from what you, sir, consider as fundamental. Confucius said, 'The superior person seeks
the roots, and when the roots are established the Way
will come forth. Filiality and fraternity make up the
roots of a human person.'"

Another teacher would say, "My path is the most
efficacious. I understand the eight hundred great points
pertaining to the body, and on top of that I can fore-
tell the future. There is no event throughout the past,
present and future that I am not aware of. You shouldn't
believe in these other teachings, but should enter upon
my path. Then you will become a living sage."

Te would reply, "I heard that Confucius said, 'To
resort to artful scheming and bizarre trickery is harm-
ful. To scandalize the world with unusual wiles is not
something that worthy ones do.' It is also said, 'The
straight mind is the Way Place.' I do not intend to
tudy this non-ultimate dharma which is a function of the
conscious mind."

When Te reached the age of eleven, I came to hear
about his virtue and filiality, and went to pay a visit
at his home. I had just entered the courtyard, when he
saw me from his window, and said to his mother, "Today
my teacher has come!"

His mother asked, "Who is your teacher?"

The boy said, "He has already come into the courtyard," and immediately went out to welcome me. It was
as if we had already known each other.

I entered the door and took a seat on the brick
bed, and chatted with him. I asked him who taught him
to bow to his parents every day. Te replied, "We have
a relative by the name of Wang, whose family lives in
Hsuang Ch'eng ("Twin Cities") County. That county alone
is known to have spawned fourteen filial sons, all of
whom adopted the practice of bowing to their parents.
Therefore, I brought forth the resolve to emulate them."

I then asked this parents what hidden virtuous acts
they had performed in order to be blessed ' th such a fil
ial offspring. His father said, "I do not recall having
done any special good acts from the moment of my birth.
Perhaps it is on account of my ancestors who have planted
blessings and virtue that we are now rewarded with such
a filial and worthy son. He causes my wife and me to be
totally without worry or distress, and our family is
very happy and free from afflictions. The Buddha's
light protects us, and our house is always as if filled
with the spring sun."

After the chat I was about to rise from my seat.
Right then Te quickly snatched away my shoes and ran and
hid them. Then he came back and knelt before me, saying,
"Today my teacher has come to Te's home. I pray that you
will grace our house and stay for lunch. I do not have
any good food to offer, but will prepare some very ordinary and simple fare." I nodded to show my consent.

After the meal I told Cheng Te to return my shoes
to me. Then I asked him, "Today you have taken refuge
with me and call me your teacher. Is it the case that
you wish to listen to your teacher's instructions, or do

you want your teacher to listen to your instructions?"

The boy answered, "Of course, I will obey my teacher's admonishments. I will rely on the teachings and offer up my conduct."

Then I said to him, "You wanted me to stay for lunch. But why did you have to first hide my shoes? That is resorting to forceful strategy and is a sign of blantant disrespect toward your teacher."

Te immediately knelt on the floor, bowed and repented, and vowed to never make the same mistake. I then taught him to specialize in cultivating the Pure Land Dharma door, to diligently spur on his three karmas, and to singlemindedly recollect the Buddha, the Dharma and the Sangha. I advised him to nourish his spirit in calmness and tranquility, and, besides attending to his school work, to use every spare moment to continually recite "Namo Amitabha" without cease.

At that time I also composed a gatha in exhortation

If in reciting the Buddha's name you can
    recite without a break,
While your mouth is reciting "Amitabha,"
    you'll become one with him.
When confused thoughts do not arise, one
    attains samadhi,
And will certainly have hopes to be
    reborn in the Pure Land.
All day long you should grow weary of
    Saha's pain,
And lessen your desires for the red dust.
Instead, strengthen your intent to
    seek rebirth in the Pure Land.
Put down defiled thoughts: just that
    is pure thought.

By reciting "Namo Amita Buddha" with
one mind, one will be transformationally
reborn from a lotus in the Western Land
of Ultimate Bliss.

ON FILIAL PIETY

As a Buddhist disciple you should cultivate the "root" Dharma-door, which is the method used to increase your good roots--"to nurture the origin and solidify the root." "To nurture the origin" means to fortify your basic energy. "To solidify the root" means to make your foundation firm.

"The origin" refers to the fundamental energy everyone needs. Everyone must be sustained by this primal energy. "The root" is filiality towards one's parents. Our parents are our origin. They gave birth to us and so we are obliged to be filial to them. If you are filial to your parents, then you are a true believer in the Buddha. If you aren't filial to your parents, then you do not truly believe in the Buddha, either. In this world take a look around you. Those who really know how to be filial to their parents wish to benefit the entire world in every move and deed and word. If people can be filial to their parents, then the righteous energy of heaven and earth will be preserved. If one isn't filial, then heaven and earth are filled with deviant energy. Being filial means being sincerely attentive and respectful towards your parents in every thought. Your parents are "living Buddhas right at home." If your parents are still living, then you have the good fortune of still being able to serve them.

Being filial means making your father and mother happy. It means doing things that please them as much as possible and avoiding doing things that pain their hearts. It means causing them to be happy at all times. In China there was a man called Lao Lai Tze, whose parents were still living when he was over eighty years old himself. He used to dress up in colorful clothes and perform for his parents as if he were a little child,

jumping around or turning somersaults to entertain his
parents and make them happy. In general, one's most
basic duty is to be filial to one's parents. If one
doesn't behave in a filial way, one has forgotten one's
roots. So any of you whose parents are still living
should be filial to them. Being filial to your parents
is much better than being filial to your teacher.

When I was in Manchuria, I was still a novice, but
a lot of people took refuge with me. Why did they take
refuge with me? They saw me as being sort of different
from most people. At that time--unusual as it may seem
--I used to walk barefoot in the snow in the dead of
winter. I didn't wear any socks or shoes. That's how
stupid I was! I paid no attention to the cold. In summer and in winter alike, I only wore three layers of
cotton clothing, and didn't wear any padded clothes.
People found it to be extraordinary that I could do that
in weather that was -34 and -35 degrees without freezing
to death. That was the reason a lot of people took
refuge with me. I had a requirement for those people
who took refuge with me in Manchuria. Every day they
had to bow to their mother and father. Since I had
bowed to my parents every day from the time I was twelve,
I thought that the people who wanted to take refuge with
me should also adopt that filial practice. The thing
that makes me happiest is for people to be filial to
their parents. Don't wait until your parents are gone,
for then it will be too late. Don't wait and end up
like the saying:

> The tree would be still,
> but the wind blows on.
> The child would be filial,
> but the parents are gone.

The tree might want to stop moving but the wind keeps

blowing and prevents it from being able to be still. The children might want to serve their parents, but their father and mother have already departed and it's too late to be filial. So be filial while you can!

If you have left home you might think, "Well, I've left the home-life and my parents aren't around, what can I do?"

Just do a good job of cultivating the Way. To do a good job at cultivating is to repay your parents' kindness. It's being filial in the utmost sense of the word. If you don't cultivate, you are letting your parents down. So those who cultivate and leave home are being filial, too. Good cultivation is filial piety. If you are a good person who doesn't do bad things and doesn't have false thinking, then you are being filial. If you are a good child, your parents will naturally receive a response in the Way, and you will thereby have fulfilled your filial duty. So it is said,

> Heaven and earth take filiality as
> important and foremost.
> If one child is filial, the whole family
> is peaceful.
> Filial children in turn give birth to
> filial children.
> And all the filial ones can become
> bright sages.

If we ourselves are filial in this ultimate sense, we can thereby influence many others to believe in the Buddhadharma. But we must truly do the work of cultivating for this response to occur. If we believe in the Buddha but just act like everyone else--eating, sleeping, wearing clothes--then we really are no different from anyone else and will not be able to influence others.

However, if we cultivate well, then our filial compliance with the Buddhas will include our parents as well.

* * *

"My brothers are older than I, and they should get the big ones. Since I am the youngest it is fitting that I receive the smallest."

A GENERAL DISCUSSION ON THE CH'AN SCHOOL

The Ch'an Sect is the leader among the Five Great Schools of Buddhism, in that it transmits the Buddha's Mind Seal, pointing directly to the mind so that one sees the nature and becomes a Buddha. When the Patriarch Bodhidharma came from India, he widely propagated this method. At that time the practitioners of Buddhism were still very enamored of literary Prajna, exerting their efforts in composition and phrasing, vying to outdo one another. Even in lecturing the Sutras they argued over long and short points, and in speaking Dharma they would praise themselves and deprecate others. Different sects were set up, and to do battle with words was the mode of the times. Some resorted to individualism, and in an attempt to be unique, they set up theories that were distinctly different from the mainstream, and perfected the art of unobstructed and clever debate. People wrote books and set up doctrines, disparaging others while advertising themselves. In this way they forsook the root and ran after the branches, and the theories of the Teaching School flourished widely.

When the Venerable Sheng Kung was slandered,[1] he retreated to Tiger Mountain and spoke Dharma to the rocks. From this came the saying that even "inert rocks knodded their heads in agreement." The Vinaya Master Tao Hsüan hid his tracks in Chung Nan Mountain, where he enjoyed food offerings of the gods. The Great Master Chih Che ("Wise One") proclaimed the Teachings, and Master Lu Shan propagated the Pure Land Method. Those who believed looked up to this, while scholars were confused by it. Everybody had a different opinion, and one was at a loss as to which way to follow. One stood perplexed at the crossroad, not knowing which way to turn. Gazing out at the vast ocean of different teachings, one heaved a big sigh.

In light of such circumstances, the First Patriarch Bodhidharma made amendments for such biased teachings and patched up the flaws. His compassionate instructions were apart from speech; his teachings were not imparted through words. He taught that this mind of ours is just the Buddha, that the precious pearl hidden within our robe is not something gotten from outside. One only needs to concentrate one's energy and refine the mind to a single focus, and in an instant one will open profuse enlightenment. At this time, the outer and inner aspects of all things, whether subtle or gross, are completely penetrated without remainder, and the great functioning of the entire substance of our minds is completely made clear. One opens vast and ultimate enlightenment, returns to the source and plumbs the origin. At this time one can appreciate the subtlety behind this interchange: the World Honored One held up a flower, Mahakashyapa, the Golden-Hued Dhuta, broke out in a smile--originally it was like this!

This method is one in which the mind seals the mind, transmitted outside of the teachings. One crosses over one's self-nature. And, after one has made one's way across the river, one leaves the raft behind. How can there be anything else but this?

1

"Icchantika" is a Sanskrit term which translates "one of insufficient faith," someone who has as much doubt as belief. If he has eight pounds of faith, for example, his doubts will also weigh eight pounds and so cancel out his faith. The first part of the NIRVANA SUTRA talked in terms of icchantikas not having the Buddha nature, and said that those of insufficient faith lacked the nature for becoming Buddhas.

At the time when only the first part of that Sutra had been translated into Chinese, Dharma Master Sheng Kung was lecturing it in Su Chou Province in China. When he came to the passage that said that icchantikas lack the Buddha Nature, he didn't explain it that way, but he said instead that they have the Buddha nature. His reasoning went like this:

"Why is it that icchantikas have the Buddha nature? It's because all living beings have the Buddha nature, and although icchantikas have insufficient faith, they are living beings. Therefore, how can one say they lack the Buddha Nature?"

He lectured it in the opposite way that the first half of the Sutra read, which outraged the other Dharma Masters of his time. They protested, "That's the talk of demon kings! The Sutra which the Buddha spoke plainly says that icchantikas don't have the Buddha nature, yet he says they do. That's really messed up." No one would have anything to do with him after that, and when he lectured Sutras no one came. The Dharma Masters ganged up and told all the disciples and good people of faith, "If Tao Sheng lectures, don't go. Anyone who listens to his Sutra lectures will fall in the hells."

Now, the whole reason the good men and women of faith were studying the Buddhadharma was so as NOT to fall into the hells. When they heard that they would fall to hell if they went to   Dharma Master Sheng Kung's Sutra lectures, they didn't dare to go listen.

Dharma Master Sheng Kung was not one to remain silent, but was determined to deliver Sutra lectures. He said, "Okay, you won't come to listen? Then I'll go lecture to the rocks and see what they do." So he went off to Hu Ch'iu Mountain and collected several hundred rocks from all over the area. He set them up in front of him and said, "I invite you to a Sutra lecture. Be good rocks and sit there nice and still." It turned out the rocks were very obedient. They didn't run off or roll away, but stayed right where he put them. When he got to the passage about icchantikas not having the Buddha nature he said, "That isn't correct. Icchantikas, too, have the Buddha nature. 'Those with and without sentience identically perfect the wisdom of all modes.' Icchantikas will become Buddhas, too. I SAID ICCHANTIKAS DO HAVE THE BUDDHA NATURE! DO YOU AGREE OR NOT?"

What do you think the rocks did then? Probably, although they were supposed to enter samadhi, they had not quite gotten into it and had not yet had a chance to fall asleep. When the rocks heard the Dharma Master ask that question, they all jumped to attention and started moving. This dull rock nodded its head, and that dull stone nodded its head. They all nodded in agreement, bumping into each other, because each would hit the rock in front of it.

Some one might wonder, "Who certified that that really happened?"It's not something the Venerable Sheng said himself. It was said by those who opposed him. How did they end up saying such a thing? Well, the reason people were against him in the first place was that he

72

lectured too well. His eloquence was unobstructed as
if lotuses were blooming on his tongue. Just about
everyone was jealous of the way he could come up with
explanations that had never occurred to anyone, and
could make Sutras come alive, as it were. That's the
way people are. If someone is better than they are,
they get jealous, and if they are better than someone
else, they look down on that person. Living beings
have that kind of knowledge and outlook, so the people
of his time formed a faction to protect against Dharma
Master Sheng Kung. When he went to the mountains to
lecture to the rocks, some of them followed him on the
sly to see what he was up to. Then he lectured to that
spot and all the rocks began to move, and without being
blown by the wind or splashed by the rain, nodded their
heads. The Dharma Masters watching from the sides who
believed in him, and even those who were against him and
were there as spies, all saw it. And that is the origin
of the saying,

> When the Venerable Sheng spoke the Dharma,
> dull rocks nodded their heads.

Afterwards, when the NIRVANA SUTRA had been completely
translated, it turned out that right in the Sutra it
says that icchantikas, too, have the Buddha nature. That
proved Dharma Master Sheng Kung had completely under-
stood the doctrine without having seen the entire Sutra,
and showed the extent of his wisdom and insight. Then,
even those who had opposed him were no longer against
him and came to bow to him. So the meaning of the dull
rocks nodding their heads is that those who had no faith
in him were the dull stones--or how could they have
failed to believe him? Yet even those who had been
jealous and against him prostrated themselves before
him.

A GENERAL DISCUSSION ON THE TEACHINGS SCHOOL

The Teachings School emphasizes using skillful
expedients, and therefore capitalizes on beautiful ex-
pressions and elegant phraseology. Adherents to this
school are well-versed in terminology and the marks.
They determine the different periods of the teachings
and divide them into categories. Thus, the sea of meanings billows, and the Dharma's principles run deep.
They serve to focus the audience's rambling thoughts,
and to gather in stray mental activities that leak out
through seeing and listening. When this occurs, it's
as if one has entered the hall of samadhi, and ascended
the heavens of the six desires. Layer upon layer one
bores in; step-by-step one ascends. Even if one wanted
to stop, it would be nearly impossible, and it's hard
to fathom the very source.

Regarding the teachings of the Teachings School--
such as the Four Teachings of T'IEN T'AI, the Five Esoteric Meanings of HSIEN SHOU, the Dharma Mark propagated
by Consciousness Only--each has its strong points. However, although each of these schools may not be biased
to the extreme, nonetheless, on occasion they extol
themselves at others' expense.

Whenever clear-eyed good knowing advisors see such
incidents they feel greatly pained at heart. Since the
foundation of the Teachings has not flourished, and
true talent is scarce, these good advisors are willing
to personally act as models, practice ascetic discipline,
and cultivate the door of the Six Paramitas. In face
of a hundred oppositions they do not bend, and they're
glad to undergo ten thousand vicissitudes, to the point
that even if their bodies had to be smashed to pieces
and their bones pulverized, they would not begrudge
such a sacrifice. Supported by magnanimous vows, they
are courageous and vigorous. Renouncing themselves for

others, they universally cross over those who have conditions. Observing the opportunities they entice with the teachings and dispense the medicine according to the illness. Not begruding weariness or toil, they would offer up their heads, eyes, brains and marrow, give away their bodies and minds, all with the sole intention of causing living beings to turn away from confusion and return to enlightenment, to cast out the deviant and come back to the proper. They want living beings to quickly attain Bodhi and perfect the sagely fruition. Therefore, they employ both provisional and actual means, and mutually bestow both sudden and gradual teachings. With kindness they draw in those with whom they have no affinities; with compassion they embrace all things and become one with them. Revealing a vast and long tongue, they take great pains to exhort with earnest words, sparing no efforts. They teach and admonish without tiring, while always conducting themselves according to strict discipline. In such ways they act as the "dragons and elephants" at the Dharma's entrance, also as teachers of gods and people. Throughout long kalpas they practice the Bodhisattva Way and never rest.

A GENERAL DISCUSSION ON THE VINAYA SCHOOL

The Vinaya School stresses the study of precepts, the rules and regulations. In the four comportments of walking, standing, sitting, and lying down, one has to be stern and dignified, and the three karmas of body, mouth, and mind have to be pure. Upasakas and Upasikas (laymen and laywomen), the two lay assemblies, maintain the Five Precepts and Eight Precepts, as well as the Ten Major and Forty-eight Minor Bodhisattva Precepts. Shramaneras and Shramanerikas take the Ten Novice Precepts. Bhikshus have 250 precepts, while bhikshunis

75

have 348 precepts. One should maintain each and every
one of those precepts without ever violating them and
believe, accept, and offer up one's conduct. One should
be mindful of the agony of revolving in birth and death.
If we lose this human body, it will be hard to recover
it in ten thousand aeons. Therefore, at all times we
should strictly cultivate the Vinaya, and never be lax.

A GENERAL DISCUSSION ON THE ESOTERIC SCHOOL

The Esoteric School specializes in holding mantras,
and purports that one can realize Buddhahood in this
very life. And yet, if practitioners are the slightest
bit reckless, they can easily fall into the Dharma Realm
of asuras. That is because the majority of those within
this practice have not subdued their minds of hatred,
and their tendency to seek revenge is extremely strong.
They lack thoughts of kindness and compassion, and rarely
practice the art of patience. Many of them are prone to
be arrogant, and their pride and conceit are deeply
rooted. In holding secret mantras they dare to slight
others, and wielding their vajras they are not afraid
of bullying people. However, if one can be rid of the
bad habits described above, then one's samadhi can come
to success, and one can go on to achieve the fruit of
Bodhi. In that case, this Dharma door is also a skillful expedient for cultivators of the Way.

A GENERAL DISCUSSION ON THE PURE LAND SCHOOL

The Pure Land School Dharma is the most perfect and
the most instantaneous, the simplest and the easiest.
It is a Dharma door that everyone can cultivate, and
one and all can practice it. Hence, it is described

as "universally including the three types of faculties (upper, middling and lower capabilities), and gathering in both the keen and dull." One only has to single-mindedly uphold the great name, "Namo Amita Buddha," the teaching host of the Land of Ultimate Bliss of the West. When one recites this name and arrives at a place of single concentration, then one will definitely be reborn in the West from a lotus flower. When that lotus blooms, one will see the Buddha, be enlightened to patience with non-production, and attain irreversibility from Anuttarasamyaksambodhi. Therefore, if all cultivators only become replete with deep faith and earnest vows, and actually realize the three requisites of Faith, Vows, and Practice, they will most certainly reach their destination. It is my hope that all of you good people will exhort each other onwards!

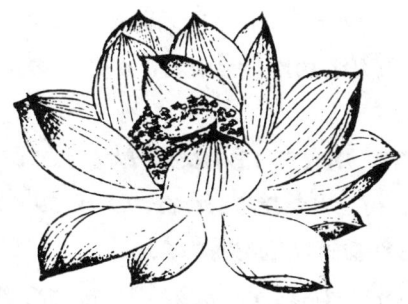

Buddhist Text Translation Society
Eight Regulations

A translator must free himself or herself from the motives of personal fame and reputation.

A translator must cultivate an attitude free from arrogance and conceit.

A translator must refrain from aggrandizing himself or herself and denigrating others.

A translator must not establish himself or herself as the standard of correctness and suppress the work of others with his or her faultfinding.

A translator must take the Buddha-mind as his or her own mind.

A translator must use the wisdom of the Selective Dharma Eye to determine true principles.

A translator must request the Elder Virtuous Ones of the ten directions to certify his or her translations.

A translator must endeavor to propagate the teachings by printing sutras, shastra texts, and vinaya texts when the translations are certified as being correct.

THE BUDDHIST TEXT TRANSLATION SOCIETY

CHAIRPERSON: The Venerable Tripitaka Master Hsüan Hua
 -Abbot of Gold Mountain Monastery,
 Gold Wheel Temple, and Tathagata Monastery
 -Chancellor of Dharma Realm Buddhist
 University
 -Professor of the Tripitaka and the Dhyanas

PRIMARY TRANSLATION COMMITTEE:

Chairpersons: Bhikshuni Heng Hsien
 Bhikshuni Heng Ch'ih

Members:

Bhikshu Heng Sure   Bhikshuni Heng Wen
Bhikshu Heng Kuan   Bhikshuni Heng Tao
Bhikshu Heng Shun   Bhikshuni Heng Jieh
Bhikshu Heng Tso   Bhikshuni Heng Ming
Bhikshu Heng Deng   Shramanerika Heng Tsai
Bhikshu Heng Kung   Shramanerika Heng Duan
Bhikshu Heng Wu   Shramanerika Heng Bin
Bhikshuni Heng Ch'ing   Shramanerika Heng Chia
Bhikshuni Heng Chü   Shramanerika Heng Liang
Bhikshuni Heng Chai   Upasaka Kuo Jung (R.B.) Epstein
Upasika Kuo Ts'an Nicholson Upasaka Kuo Li (Li-jen) Chou
Upasaka Kuo Chou Rounds

REVIEWING COMMITTEE:

Chairpersons: Bhikshu Heng Tso
 Upasaka Kuo Jung Epstein

Members:

Bhikshu Heng Sure   Bhikshuni Heng Chai
Bhikshu Heng Kuan   Bhikshuni Heng Wen
Bhikshu Heng Deng   Bhikshuni Heng Tao
Bhikshu Heng Gung   Shramanerika Heng Tsai
Bhikshu Heng Wu   Shramanerika Heng Duan
Bhikshuni Heng Hsien   Upasaka Kuo Jung Epstein
Bhikshuni Heng Ch'ih   Upasika Hsien Ping-ying
Upasika Kuo Ts'an Nicholson Upasaka Kuo Chou Rounds
Upasika Kuo Chin Vickers   Upasaka Chou Kuo Li
Upasika Phuong Kuo Wu

EDITING COMMITTEE:

Chairperson: Upasika Kuo Tsai Rounds

Advisor: Bhikshu Heng Kuan

Members:

Bhikshu Heng Sure
Bhikshu Heng Lai
Bhikshu Heng Shun
Bhikshu Heng Ch'au
Bhikshu Heng Tso
Bhikshu Heng Ch'i
Bhikshu Heng Wu
Bhikshuni Heng Hsien
Bhikshuni Heng Ch'ih
Bhikshuni Heng Ch'ing
Bhikshuni Heng Chü
Upasaka Kuo Jung Epstein
Upasaka Kuo Tsun (Randall
  Dinwiddie
Upasaka Kuo Chou Rounds
Upasika Kuo Ts'ung Dinwiddie
Upasika Kuo Lin (Nancy)
  Lethcoe

Bhikshuni Heng Chai
Bhikshuni Heng Wen
Bhikshuni Heng Tao
Bhikshuni Heng Jieh
Bhikshuni Heng Ming
Shramanera Heng Jau
Shramanerika Heng Tsai
Shramanerika Heng Duan
Shramanerika Heng Bin
Shramanerika Heng Chia
Shramanerika Heng Liang
Upasika Kuo Ts'an Nicholson
Upasika Chou Kuo Li
Upasika Phuong Kuo Wu
Upasika Kuo Chin Vickers
Upasaka Kuo Lei Powers

CERTIFYING COMMITTEE:

Chairperson: Venerable Tripitaka Master Hsüan Hua

Members:

Bhikshu Heng Sure
Bhikshu Heng Kuan
Bhikshu Heng Tso
Bhikshuni Heng Hsien
Upasaka Wong Kuo Chün
Upasika Kuo Ts'an Nicholson

Bhikshuni Heng Ch'ih
Bhikshuni Heng Ch'ing
Bhikshuni Heng Wen
Bhikshuni Heng Tao

Upasaka Kuo Jung Epstein
Upasika Kuo Chin Vickers

CHINESE PUBLICATIONS COMMITTEE:

Chairperson: Upasaka Chou Kuo Li

Members:

Shramanerika Kuo Hua
Upasika Phuong Kuo Wu
Upasika Kuo Han Epstein

Dharma Protector Wei T'o Bodhisattva

Verse of Transference

May the merit and virtue accrued from this work,
Adorn the Buddhas' Pure Lands,
Repaying four kinds of kindness above,
And aiding those suffering in the paths below.

May those who see and hear of this,
All bring forth the resolve for Bodhi,
And when this retribution body is over,
Be born together in ultimate bliss.

Publications from the
Buddhist Text Translation Society

All BTTS translations include extensive inter-linear commentary by the Venerable Tripitaka Master Hsuan Hua, unless otherwise noted. All works available in softcover only unless otherwise noted.
ISBN Prefix: 0-917512

SUTRAS (Scriptures spoken by the Buddha):

AMITABHA SUTRA - Explains the causes and circumstances for rebirth in the Land of Ultimate Bliss of Amitabha Buddha. 01-4, 204 pgs., $8.00. (Also available in Spanish. $8.00)

BRAHMA NET SUTRA - Vol. I contains the Ten Major Precepts, and the first Twenty Minor Precepts. English/Chinese. 79-0, 300 pgs., $10.00.
Vol. II - The Twenty-first Minor Precept through the Forty-Eighth Minor Precept. English/Chinese. 88-X, 210 pgs., $8.00.
Entire text only is also available. 56-1, $5.00.

DHARANI SUTRA - Tells of the past events in the life of the Bodhisattva of Great Compassion, Avalokiteshvara (Kuan Yin). It explains the meaning of the mantra line by line, and contains Chinese poems and drawings of division bodies of Kuan Yin for each of the 84 lines of the mantra. Drawings and verses on each of the 42 Hands and Eyes of Kuan Yin. 13-8, 352 pgs., $12.00.

千手千眼大悲心陀羅尼經 - **DHARANI SUTRA** - Original Chinese text only. 210 pgs., $6.00.

DHARMA FLOWER (LOTUS) SUTRA- This Sutra, spoken in the last period of the Buddha's teaching, proclaims the ultimate principles of the Dharma which unites all previous teachings into one. The following are volumes which have been published to date:
VOL. I INTRODUCTION.
VOL. II INTRODUCTION, CHAPTER ONE.
VOL. III EXPEDIENT METHODS, CHAPTER TWO.
VOL. IV A PARABLE, CHAPTER THREE.
VOL. V BELIEF AND UNDERSTANDING, CHAPTER FOUR.
VOL. VI MEDICINAL HERBS, CHAPTER FIVE, and CONFERRING PREDICTIONS, CHAPTER SIX.
VOL. VII PARABLE OF THE TRANSFORMATION CITY, CHAPTER SEVEN.
VOL. VIII FIVE HUNDRED DISCIPLES RECEIVE PREDICTIONS, CHAPTER EIGHT, and BESTOWING PREDICTIONS UPON THOSE STUDYING AND BEYOND STUDY, CHAPTER NINE.
VOL. IX THE DHARMA MASTER, CHAPTER TEN, and VISION OF THE JEWELED STUPA, CHAPTER 11.

VOL. X DEVADATTA, CHAPTER TWELVE. Coming Soon.

FLOWER ADORNMENT (AVATAMSAKA) SUTRA VERSE PREFACE
清涼國師 華嚴經序淺釋) a succinct verse commentary by T'ang Dynasty National Master Ch'ing Liang (the Master of seven emperors), which gives a complete overview of all the fundamental principles contained in the Sutra in eloquent style. First English translation. BI-LINGUAL EDITION Chinese and English. 244 pgs., 28-6, $7.00.

FLOWER ADORNMENT SUTRA PROLOGUE. A detailed explanation of the principles of the Sutra utilizing the Hsien Shou method of analyzing scriptures known as the Ten Doors, by National Master Ch'ing Liang. The following volumes have been published to date:

*VOL. I, THE FIRST DOOR: THE CAUSES AND CONDITIONS
FOR THE ARISAL OF THE TEACHING.   252 pgs., p.66-9
$10.00.
VOL. II, THE SECOND DOOR: THE STORES AND TEACHINGS
TO WHICH IT BELONGS.   PART ONE. 280 pgs., 73-1,
$10.00.*

清淨國師 華嚴經疏浅浅釋   entirety of the AVATAMSAKA SUTRA
PROLOGUE, from First to Tenth Door, together with inter-
linear commentary by Ven. Abbot Hua, in four Volumes.
CHINESE $5.00, $8.50, $8.50, and $5.00.

FLOWER ADORNMENT SUTRA - Known as the king of kings of
all Buddhist scriptures because of its great length,
(81 rolls containing more than 700,000 Chinese charac-
ters), and its profundity; it contains the most complete
explanation of the Buddha's state and the Bodhisattva's
quest for Awakening. When completed, the entire Sutra
text with commentary is estimated to be from 75 to 100
volumes. The following volumes have been published to
date:

> *FLOWER STORE SEA OF ADORNED WORLDS, CHAPTER 5,
> PART I. Available Soon.
> BRIGHT ENLIGHTENMENT, CHAPTER 9. Available Soon.
> PURE CONDUCT, CHAPTER 11. Available Soon.
> TEN DWELLINGS, CHAPTER 15. 77-4, 185 pgs., $8.00.
> BRAHMA CONDUCT, CHAPTER 16. 80-4, 65 pgs., $4.00.
> THE MERIT AND VIRTUE FROM FIRST BRINGING FORTH
> THE MIND, CHAPTER 17. 83-9, 200 pgs., $7.00.
> TEN INEXHAUSTIBLE TREASURIES, CHAPTER 22. 38-3,
> 184 pgs., $7.00.
> PRAISES IN THE TUSHITA HEAVEN PALACE, CHAPTER 24.
> 39-1.
> TEN TRANSFERENCES, CHAPTER 25, PART I. Available Soon.
> TEN GROUNDS, CHAPTER 26, PART I. 87-1, 234 pgs,$7.00.
> TEN GROUNDS, CHAPTER 26, PART II. 74-X, 200 pgs.,
> $8.00.*

華嚴經十地品浅釋   The Second to the Tenth Grounds,
contains the Bodhisattva's successive certification to
each of the Sagely Grounds. CHINESE only. Grounds Two
to Five in one volume now available; remaining Grounds
forthcoming.

ENTERING THE DHARMA REALM, CHAPTER 39. This chapter
relates the spiritual journey of the Youth Good Wealth
in his search for Ultimate Awakening. In his quest he
meets fifty-three "Good Teachers," each of whom represents a successive stage on the Bodhisattva path. The
following volumes have been published to date:

> PART I.   Describes the setting for the Youth's quest,
> and his meeting with Manjushri Bodhisattva.   280 pgs.,
> 68-5, $8.50.

> PART 2.   Good Wealth meets his first ten teachers,
> who represent the positions of the Ten Dwellings.
> 250 pgs., 73-1, $8.50.

> PART 3.   The ten teachers who correspond to the
> levels of the Ten Conducts.   250 pgs., 73-1, $8.50.

> PART 4.   The ten teachers who represent the First
> to Sixth Grounds.   300 pgs., 81-2, $9.00.

> PART 5.   The four teachers who represent the Seventh
> to Tenth Grounds of a Bodhisattva.   Available Decem-
> ber, 1982.

HEART SUTRA AND VERSES WITHOUT A STAND - The text explains the meaning of Prajna Paramita, the perfection of
wisdom. Each line in the Sutra is accompanied by an
eloquent verse by the Ven. Abbot Hua. 160 pgs., 28-7,
$7.50.

般若波羅蜜多心經非台頌解   same as above, including
the commentary. IN CHINESE. 120 pgs., $5.00.

SHURANGAMA SUTRA - This Sutra, which reveals the Shurangama Samadhi and which contains the Shurangama Mantra,
primarily concerns the mind.
> *VOL. I.* Seven locations of the mind are all refuted.
> 289 pgs., 17-0, $8.50.
> *VOL. II.* Ten aspects of seeing; individual and col-
> lective karma. 212 pgs., 25-1, $8.50.
> *VOL. III.* Six sense organs, objects and conscious-
> nesses and seven elements. 240 pgs., 94-4, $8.50.
> *VOL. IV.* Continuity of world, living beings and
> karmic retribution. 200 pgs., 90-1, $8.50.
> *VOL. V.* Twenty-five sages tell of their perfect pene-
> tration. Kuan Yin Bodhisattva's method is selected
> by Manjushri Bodhisattva as most appropriate for peo-
> ple in this world. 250 pgs., 91-X, $8.50.

SHRAMANERA VINAYA AND RULES OF DEPORTMENT - This text,
by Great Master Lien Ch'ih of the Ming Dynasty, explains
the moral code for Shramaneras (novice monks). 112 pgs.,
04-9, $4.00.

沙門崇行錄 An ancient text compiled by Great Master
Lien Ch'ih of the Ming Dynasty, on the Vinaya (moral
code) for Bhikshus. No commentary. CHINESE. 130 pgs.

SHURANGAMA MANTRA COMMENTARY -Explains how to practice
the foremost mantra in the Buddha's teaching, including
a line by line analysis of the mantra. BILINGUAL,
Chinese and English. 69-3, $8.50.
> *VOL. 2.* Contains a verse and commentary to explain
> lines 30 to 90 of the mantra. English/Chinese. 82-0,
> 200 pgs., $7.50.
> *VOL. 3.* *Available Soon.*

SONG OF ENLIGHTENMENT - The lyric poem of the state of
the Ch'an sage, by T'ang Dynasty Master Yung Chia.
AVAILABLE SOON.

永嘉大師證道歌詮釋, same as above with commentary
by the Ven. Abbot Hua. CHINESE. 40 pgs., $2.50.

宣化上人偈讚開釋錄, Verses by the Ven. Abbot Hua.
IN CHINESE. 73 pgs., $5.00.

THE TEN DHARMA REALMS ARE NOT BEYOND A SINGLE THOUGHT.
An eloquent poem on all the realms of being, which is
accompanied by extensive commentarial material and drawings. 72 pgs., 12-X, $4.00.

BIOGRAPHICAL:

> *PICTORIAL BIOGRAPHY OF VENERABLE MASTER HSÜ YÜN, Vol.
> I.* *Available Soon.*

RECORDS OF THE LIFE OF THE VENERABLE MASTER HSÜAN HUA.
The life and teachings of the Ven. Abbot from his birth-
place in China, to the present time in America.
> *VOL. I* - covers the Abbot's life in China. 96 pgs.,
> 07-3, $5.00. ALSO IN SPANISH, $8.00.
> *VOL. II* - covers the events of the Abbot's life as he
> cultivated and taught his followers in Hong Kong. This
> volume contains many photos, poems and stories. 229 pgs.,
> 10-3, $8.00.

宣化禪師事蹟 - same as above, Volumes I and II.
IN CHINESE. 94 pgs., $6.00.

THREE STEPS, ONE BOW - The daily journal of American
Bhikshus Heng Ju and Heng Yo, who in 1973-74 made a re-
ligious pilgrimage from Gold Mountain Monastery in San
Francisco to Marblemount, Washington, bowing every third
step on their way. 160 pgs., 18-9, $5.95.

WORLD PEACE GATHERING - A collection of instructional
talks on Buddhism commemorating the successful comple-
tion of the bowing pilgrimage of Bhikshus Heng Ju and
Heng Yo. 128 pgs., 05-7, $5.00.

WITH ONE HEART BOWING TO THE CITY OF 10,000 BUDDHAS -
The moving journals of American Bhikshus Heng Sure and
Heng Ch'au, who made a "three steps, one bow" pilgrimage from Gold Wheel Temple in Los Angeles to the City
of 10,000 Buddhas, located 110 miles north of San Francisco, from May,1977 to October, 1979.

> *VOL. 1* - May 6 to June 30, 1977; 180 pgs., 21-9,$6.00.
> *VOL. 11* - July 1 to October 30, 1977; 322 pgs, 23-5,
> $7.50.
> *VOL. 111*- October 30 to December 16, 1977; 154 pgs.,
>   89-8, $6.00.
> *VOL. 1V* - December 17, 1977 to January 21, 1978; 136
>   pgs., 90-1, $5.00.
> *VOL. V* - January 22 to February 18, 1978; 127 pgs.,
>   91-X, $5.00.
> *VOL. V1* - February 19, 1978 to April 2, 1978; 200 pgs.,
>   92-8, $6.00.
> *VOL. VII* -April 3, 1978 to May 24, 1978; 168 pgs.;
>   99-5.

Other volumes to appear in sequence, including the
journals from the continuation of "Three Steps One
Bow" within the City of 10,000 Buddhas, still in
progress to date.

修行者的消息· - *NEWS FROM TWO CULTIVATORS - LETTERS
OF THREE STEPS, ONE BOW.* The letters from Dharma Masters Heng Sure and Heng Ch'au chronicling the entirety
of their 2 1/2 year journey to reach the City of 10,000
Buddhas. CHINESE only. $7.00.

HENG CH'AU'S JOURNAL - An account of the remarkable ex-
periences and changes undergone by Bhikshu Heng Ch'au
when he first became acquainted with Gold Mountain Monastery. $1.95.

OPEN YOUR EYES, TAKE A LOOK AT THE WORLD - The journals
of Bhikshus Heng Sure and Heng Ch'au and Bhikshuni Heng
Tao, taken during the 1978 Asia-region visit by the Ven.
Abbot Hua together with other members of the Sino-American Buddhist Association. 347 pgs., 32-4, $7.50.

放眼觀世界--亞州弘法記 - the above, in Chinese.
347 pgs., $7.50.

MUSIC, NOVELS, AND BROCHURES:

THREE CART PATRIARCH - A 12" stereo LP recorded by and
for children, based on the Monkey Tales of China.
$7.00 plus $1.00 shipping.

CITY OF 10,000 COLOR BROCHURE - Over 30 color photos of
the center of World Buddhism located in the scenic Men-
docino County near Wonderful Enlightenment Mountain.
24 pgs., $2.00.

CELEBRISI'S JOURNEY - David Round's novel describing
the events in a modern American's quest for enlightenment.
178 pgs., 14-6, $4.00.

VAJRA BODHI SEA 萬佛城. A monthly journal of ortho-
dox Buddhism published by the Sino-American Buddhist
Association since 1970. Each issue contains the most
recent translation work of the Buddhist Text Translation
Society, as well as a biography of a great Patriarch of
Buddhism from the ancient past, sketches of the lives
of contemporary monastic and lay followers from around
the world, a Sanskrit lesson, scholarly articles, and
other material. The journal is BILINGUAL in Chinese
and English in an 8 1/2" by 11" format. Single issues
$2.00, one year $22.00, and three years $60.00.

POSTAGE AND HANDLING:

United States: $1.00 for the first book and 40¢ for each additional book. All publications are sent via special fourth class. Allow 4 days to 2 weeks for delivery.

International: $1.25 for the first book and 75¢ for each additional book. All publications are sent via "book rate." We recommend that for orders of approximately 10 or more, an additional $3.00 per parcel of 100 books be sent for registration to protect against loss. We are not responsible for parcels lost in the mail.

All orders require pre-payment before they will be processed.

PUBLICATIONS AVAILABLE AT:

GOLD MOUNTAIN MONASTERY   (415) 861-9672
1731-15th Street.
San Francisco, CA. 94103

THE CITY OF 10,000 BUDDHAS   (707) 462-0939
Box 217
Talmage, CA. 95481

GOLD WHEEL TEMPLE   (213) 483-7497
1728 West Sixth Street
Los Angeles, CA. 90017

中文佛書目錄

中美佛教總會法界大學出版

經典部分：

① 大方廣佛華嚴經序淺釋（漢英對照） 美國萬佛城宣化上人講解，全一冊。定價美金七元。

② 大方廣佛華嚴經疏淺釋（平裝四冊） 美國萬佛城宣化上人講解。

第一冊（第一門，敎起因緣） 定價美金五元。

第二冊（第二門，藏敎所攝） 定價美金八元五角。

第三冊（第三門，義理分齊。第四門，敎所被機。第五門，敎體淺深。第六門，宗趣通別）
定價美金八元五角。

第四冊（第七門，部類品會。第八門，傳譯感通。第九門，總釋名題。第十門，別解文義）
定價美金五元。

③ 大方廣佛華嚴經淺釋（平裝八冊） 美國萬佛城宣化上人講解。

第一冊（世主妙嚴品第一，卷一至卷二） 定價美金七元。

第二冊（世主妙嚴品第一，卷三） 定價美金五元。

第三冊（世主妙嚴品第一，卷四至卷五） 定價美金七元。

第四冊（如來現相品第二。普賢三昧品第三。世界成就品第四） 定價美金五元。

第五冊（華藏世界品第五。毗盧遮那品第六。如來名號品第七。四聖諦品第八）
定價美金七元。

第六冊（光明覺品第九。菩薩問明品第十。淨行品第十一） 定價美金七元。

第七冊（賢首品第十二。升須彌山頂品第十三。須彌頂山偈讚第十四。十住品第十五）
定價美金七元。

第八冊（梵行品第十六。初發心功德品第十七。明法品第十八。升夜摩天品第十九。夜摩偈讚品第二十） 定價美金五元。

佛書部分：

① 永嘉大師證道歌詮釋（全一冊）　美國萬佛城宣化上人講解　定價美金二元五角。

② 緇門崇行錄　蓮池大師著　弘一大師集　（贈閱）

③ 宣化上人偈讚聞釋錄（全一冊）　定價美金五元　（贈閱）

④ 宣化禪師事蹟（全一冊）　定價美金四元。

⑤ 放眼觀世界（亞洲弘法記）　（全一冊）　（贈閱）

⑥ 修行者的消息（三步一拜兩行者一心頂禮萬佛城之來鴻）　（贈閱）

⑦ 佛教精進者的日記　（平裝上冊）　定價美金六元。

⑧ 萬佛城雜誌月刊（漢英合刊）　定價一年美金二十二元。三年美金六十元。

即將出版：

① 大方廣佛華嚴經淺釋（十定品至入法界品）

② 楞嚴咒疏句偈解（漢英對照）　（第二冊）

③ 梵網經講錄（漢英對照）　（下冊）

④ 地藏菩薩本願經淺釋

⑤ 大佛頂首楞嚴經淺釋

⑥ 沙彌律儀淺釋

⑦ 佛教精進者的日記（下冊）

⑧ 宣化上人語錄

⑨ 萬佛城聯語集

總流通處：中美佛教總會金山寺

Gold mt. Monastery 1731 15th St. San Francisco, CA.94103 U.S.A.

南無阿彌陀佛

南無觀世音菩薩

南無大勢至菩薩

聖作三方西
行其惡諸
慧奉善眾
救其淨自
佛諸是

④大方廣佛華嚴經十地品淺釋（平裝三冊）　美國萬佛城宣化上人講解。

第一冊（第一歡喜地）（漢英對照）　定價美金七元。

第二冊（第二離垢地。第三發光地。第四燄慧地。第五難勝地）　定價美金五元。

第三冊（第六現前地。第七遠行地。第八不動地。第九善慧地。第十法雲地）定價美金六元

⑤千手千眼大悲心陀羅尼經（全一冊）　定價美金六元。

⑥般若波羅蜜多心經非台頌解（全一冊）　美國萬佛城宣化上人講解　定價美金五元。

⑦楞嚴咒疏句偈解（漢英對照）（第一冊）　美國萬佛城宣化上人講解　定價美金八元五角。

⑧梵網經講錄（漢英對照）（上冊）　慈僧法師述　定價美金十元。